Feasts of
Good Fortune

FEASTS OF GOOD FORTUNE

75 Recipes for a Year of Chinese American Celebrations, from Lunar New Year to Mid-Autumn Festival and Beyond

By HSIAO-CHING CHOU & MEILEE CHOU RIDDLE

Photography by CLARE BARBOZA

 SASQUATCH BOOKS | SEATTLE

Printed in South Korea

SASQUATCH BOOKS with colophon is a registered trademark of Penguin Random House LLC

28 27 26 25 24   9 8 7 6 5 4 3 2 1

Editor: Jill Saginario
Production editor: Peggy Gannon
Designer: Tony Ong
Photographer: Clare Barboza
(Page 124 dragon boat photo © kingrobert/adobe.com)
(Page 159 winter photo © Francisco Little/adobe.com)
(Page 224 hot pot photo: Scott Eklund)
Styling: Clare Barboza and Hsiao-Ching Chou

Library of Congress Cataloging-in-Publication Data
Names: Chou, Hsiao-Ching, 1972- author. | Riddle, Meilee Chou, author. | Barboza, Clare, photographer. Title: Feasts of good fortune : 75 recipes for a year of Chinese American celebrations, from Lunar New Year to Mid-Autumn Festival and beyond. Hsiao-Ching Chou, Meilee Chou Riddle; photography by Clare Barboza. Description: Seattle, WA : Sasquatch Books, [2024] | Includes bibliographical references and index.
Identifiers: LCCN 2024009794 | ISBN 9781632175182 (paperback) | ISBN   9781632175199 (ebook) Subjects: LCSH: Cooking, Chinese. | LCGFT: Cookbooks. Classification: LCC TX724.5.C5 C57192 2024 | DDC 641.5951–dc23/eng/20240312.
LC record available at https://lccn.loc.gov/2024009794

The recipes contained in this book have been created for the ingredients and techniques indicated. Neither publisher nor author is responsible for your specific health or allergy needs that may require supervision. Nor are publisher and author responsible for any adverse reactions you may have to the recipes contained in the book, whether you follow them as written or modify them to suit your personal dietary needs or tastes.

ISBN: 978-1-63217-518-2

Sasquatch Books
1325 Fourth Avenue, Suite 1025
Seattle, WA 98101

SasquatchBooks.com

FSC
www.fsc.org

MIX
Paper | Supporting
responsible forestry
FSC® C140526

For Meilee: May this experience anchor you to our love for you.

—HSIAO-CHING CHOU

To my cousins, my built-in companions, whose presence has made life's journey all the more laughter-filled and meaningful.

—MEILEE RIDDLE

Table of Contents

Connecting with Chinese Traditions

PART 2:
Celebrating Our Mixed Culture

Why This Book

MOM SAYS

"When can we get together with the cousins again?" My daughter's voice was filled with longing for a family dinner we wouldn't be able to host for an unknowable period of time. Lunar New Year, birthdays, Thanksgiving, Christmas, all the celebrations that mark the passing of the year suddenly changed shape when a virus shut down the world. What we valued about the togetherness of a shared meal sharpened when the ability to gather evaporated.

As a parent, I never know what practices and traditions stick with my two kids and their five cousins. Teenagers are especially inscrutable. So Meilee's wish for dinner with our extended family broke my heart because I didn't know how long the pandemic would restrict our lives. And it also signaled that all the past dinners had imprinted their memories in her consciousness. In a painful moment, I found hope—and the seed for this book. I can share recipes and their stories through the recipe headnotes. But passing on traditions requires someone to receive them with intention. It's also the responsibility of the bearer to invite the next generation into the narrative, to make space for the perspectives of those who will carry on our histories.

Conversations with Meilee taught me that she and her Asian peers constantly grapple with bias in subtle and blatant ways, struggle with their mixed-race identities, and are figuring out their social justice voices. In the midst of the fight, food is where they meet to find joy and deliciousness. Co-creating this book with Meilee means she can find herself in the story and explore future evolutions of herself without fear of losing her way. Meilee, her brother, Shen, and all their cousins are mixed-race. The experiences of this generation of young people and how they bond through food are important to how we talk about celebrations.

The phrase in Mandarin, 團圓, or "tuan yuan" (tuan = together and yuan = round or circle), signifies the act of coming together for a family meal, especially around the holidays. *Feasts of Good Fortune* is about tuan yuan meals and the roundness they bring to families and friends. I've featured Lunar New Year menus in both *Chinese Soul Food* and *Vegetarian Chinese Soul Food* but haven't gone beyond that to share the symbolic foods and traditions of other holidays. If my first two books were "on-ramps" to everyday Chinese home cooking, this book on celebrations completes the story.

We also want to acknowledge that how we honor traditional holidays is very much influenced by where we live. I was born in Taipei, Taiwan, but I grew up in the United States in the Midwest, and I've now lived more than twenty years in Seattle, Washington. Meilee was born in Seattle and has grown up in this place known for wild salmon, Dungeness crab, and roadside blackberry brambles. She can dispatch a Dungeness crab with stunning swiftness! Our culture and family are forever hyphenated and so are many of the ingredients we use to make the foods we like.

The older I get, the farther away I feel from the place where I was born. That distance morphed my relationship to traditions my parents used to practice when my brothers and I were kids. I have to reach deep into my memory banks to connect with moments where

MEILEE'S PERSPECTIVE: A YEAR IN THE LIFE OF MY FAMILY

In our Chinese American family, every year holds countless celebrations big and small. These celebrations aren't just dates on a calendar; they're the moments that will stick with us forever. No matter the time of year, our home is filled with the flavors, sights, and sounds of both Chinese and American traditions. I'd like to tell you about a year in our house and just a few of our celebrations, from Lunar New Year's vibrant red lanterns to Thanksgiving's huge feast.

We begin every January ringing in the new year with our latest goals and resolutions, trying to start it off on the right track. My dad cleans up the house and makes sure we start things organized while my brother and I grasp to our last few days off from school.

Lunar New Year typically falls between mid-January and mid-February. Lunar New Year is probably one of the biggest celebrations of the year. Preparation begins at least a week in advance. My mom begins planning a menu, making sure she hits everyone's favorites. Then she and my grandma head to the local Asian market. To paint a picture for those who are unfamiliar, imagine grocery stores around Thanksgiving or Christmas. It's intense. Lots of the elderly Asian people are up bright and early to stock up on everything from meats to vegetables to red envelopes and decorations. Everyone is on their own mission to create a feast to start the new year off right. My mom starts cooking a few days in advance.

March and April mark the changing seasons. We celebrate the beauty of the Pacific Northwest as it transitions. I am very lucky to live in an area surrounded by nature. I can look out my window every day and see the trees changing, hear birds chirping, and smell the salty bay.

In our extended family, we have at least three birthdays in May. My mom always marks her birthday with a classic chocolate cake. Whether I make it for her or we order it from a fancy bakery, she is content regardless. My brother likes to spend his birthday with his friends. Each year, the celebration gets more and more high-tech. He evolves with technology. The last birthday in May is my cousin Lucie's. For most birthdays on my mom's side of the family, we default to a night out at Din Tai Fung. Our buzzing group of thirteen fills the restaurant to the brim with love, laughter, and memories.

June is the end of school! My brother and I are always excited and ready to embrace summertime and the freedom that comes along with it. On top of that, my lau lau's ("lau lau" describes the maternal grandmother) birthday falls on a different day every year depending on the lunar calendar. I admire how she lives her life simply: wake up, garden, take photos of plants, write her blog, watch Asian dramas on YouTube, sleep, repeat. She doesn't mind the simplicity after a long life full of beautiful chaos.

we honored our ancestors or picked through our favorite mooncake flavors. Lunar New Year has always been the main holiday, filled with pomp. Without intention, holidays can become afterthoughts, and I don't want that to be the case. So here we are. I hope *Feasts of Good*

Fortune is a reminder of the moments we have throughout the year to come together. And that it bridges the nostalgia with the futures that live in my kids and their peers.

—HSIAO-CHING CHOU

Each Fourth of July, my dad's side of the family comes together at my aunt Julene's cozy Camano Island cabin. My uncle Joe, who's married to Julene, guides us as we embark on our crabbing expedition to catch our feast for the night. We look out onto the waters, trying to find the buoys until, finally, the vibrant green and orange stripes catch our eye. After pulling on the rope for what feels like ages, our bounty of crab emerges. We boil the freshly caught crabs and serve them alongside sizzling steaks and plenty of sides. The meal sets the stage for a memorable Fourth of July tradition, complete with neighborhood fireworks to light up the night.

September is a busy month. My brother and I go back to school, which is always chaos. We are bombarded with back-to-school forms and the ache of getting up early in the morning. My parents celebrate their anniversary, and shortly after is my dad's birthday (he hates getting older). September also marks the Mid-Autumn Festival. My mom and grandma will bring home mooncakes from our local Asian grocery store. We don't eat a ton of them or celebrate too extravagantly for that matter. But we do have our mooncakes and recognize being together and being thankful for the things we have brought into our lives.

October is the beginning of the American holiday season. My birthday is October 3, so it is always nice to celebrate my day. In my family we pick a restaurant to go to for birthday dinners and

I typically pick Asian or Italian food. Halloween is always a fun celebration. No matter how old I am, I have a lot of fun dressing up and creating costumes. It's something I have loved to do my whole life—not to mention having candy all night, which is a treat for anyone.

November is known as a month to be thankful. Around Thanksgiving, my family and I head up to Whistler to meet with family friends. We aren't big skiers, but playing in the snow is an infrequent activity in Seattle, so we do like to take advantage of Whistler's slopes. For Thanksgiving dinner, each family brings their favorite dishes, and we all cram into the Woodman family's hotel room for the potluck. We never stick to a specific kind of food: the past few years, it has been a mix of turkey and sides; or bo ssam (Korean-style pork shoulder), rice, and lettuce wraps. Not exactly traditional, but delicious.

The final celebrations wrap up in December. Christmas also happens to be my yeh yeh's (grandpa Claude Riddle's) birthday. He's my dad's dad, and he has lived a very long and full life. On Christmas 2023, he turned 100. Soon after Christmas comes New Year's Eve. It's a time to reflect on the past year. I love being able to look back at all the memories I have made over the years. Celebrations big and small, they're all meaningful for me.

Introduction

Welcome and hello! Let's ground ourselves first. Yes, *Feasts of Good Fortune* is about the holidays and events we celebrate in our Chinese American home, and we've categorized recipes accordingly. But you can make these dishes when you feel like it and in whatever combination you'd like. We're not going to be precious about it. The Stir-Fried Romaine (page 66) or Garlic Shrimp with Gai Lan (page 69), for example, are great anytime. In fact, 95 percent of the dishes in this book might appear on our table on a given weeknight. So feel free to use this as an everyday cookbook as much as a reference for a few major Chinese holidays.

Why are we starting here? Because we're human. We all sometimes feel like we need permission to stray from generations of cultural practice—or the printed word. We're forgiving of ourselves for not following traditions to the letter and, by whatever power our position grants us, we extend to you the same consideration. We want joy and deliciousness in the kitchen, not baggage and guilt.

At the end of the day, what's most important about any celebration is the act of getting together to honor the moment and the people present—or those who have passed—and to share a bite. There are any number of factors that can affect how you celebrate: maybe it's a lean year and you don't have a lot of resources to afford an extravagant feast; maybe you can't travel to be with your people and you have to raise a toast from afar; perhaps schedules don't align and you have to postpone your gathering. Whatever the circumstances, there's a way to mark the day without putting the pressure on you and yours to make it "perfect." This is most definitely not that kind of book. If you have the capacity to make it all, go for it! If you use this book as nothing more than a guide and end up buying all the foods from a nearby Chinese restaurant, you will get no judgment from us. You do you.

For this book, we want to be clear that our perspective is a kaleidoscope. Turn it one way, you get our family's Chinese roots. Turn it again, you'll taste Taiwan. A few more degrees around the scope, and the Pacific Northwest shows up. Freedom threads itself throughout our recipes— to experiment, to be resourceful, to be true to your circumstances. Dare we say that the instinct to do as we wish is very much American? We've always believed in making it easier for people to connect with our culture. Wade into some of the traditions with us, and if you want to go deeper, there are many excellent books that will guide you into the thousands of years of cuisines and culture of China, Taiwan, and the diaspora.

THE CALENDAR

To situate yourself around the ebb and flow of the holidays we talk about in this book, you'll need to have a basic understanding of the lunisolar calendar. This is different from the "regular" or Gregorian calendar that we're all used to. It's a common mistake to describe the Chinese calendar as a lunar calendar—we've referred to the lunar calendar for as long as we can remember. It's technically the lunisolar calendar, which follows the moon phases and the time of the solar year. The lunisolar calendar consists of twelve to thirteen months, with a leap month every several years to keep it from falling too far behind the Gregorian calendar. Strictly following the lunar cycles would eventually create too much of a discrepancy with the Gregorian calendar.

According to the famous Theodora Lau in her classic *The Handbook of Chinese Horoscopes*, the lunisolar calendar originated in 2637 BCE during the reign of Emperor Huangdi—the Yellow Emperor—who was known for uniting many warring tribes and ushering in a new age of civilization.

In 2023, there was a leap month and the lunar second month repeated. (In 2020, the fourth month repeated and Lau Lau—Meilee's grandma—got to celebrate her seventy-eighth birthday twice!) Each month begins when the moon lines up with the earth and the sun. There are twenty-nine or thirty days in each month. Historically, this calendar was like an almanac

and helped to guide farmers on when to plant their crops. It was also used to help set wedding dates and other milestones, such as when to start a new project or when to travel. As a result, all the festivals and holidays follow the lunisolar calendar. To know when a holiday takes place, you need to know how to read a Chinese calendar. Or do what we do and search online for the date of a given holiday.

The dates of the holidays we cover are listed in this way:

LUNAR NEW YEAR: First Day, First Month

LANTERN FESTIVAL: Fifteenth Day, First Month

QINGMING FESTIVAL: Fifth Day, Fourth Month

DRAGON BOAT FESTIVAL: Fifth Day, Fifth Month

MID-AUTUMN FESTIVAL: Fifteenth Day, Eighth Month

On the conversion chart on page 8, you can get a sense of the Gregorian calendar next to the lunisolar calendar dates.

TO MAKE IT OR BUY IT

For those who *love* to cook, the holidays can be energizing. It's when we obsess about a menu, make lists of ingredients, and spend days preparing. The meal becomes a way to convey love, generosity, and all the warmth that comes with the territory. We take great pleasure in knowing that our extended family members look forward to dinner at our home. But for those who cook only occasionally—or not particularly well—and who suddenly want to cook during the holidays, trying to make *everything* may not be wise.

There's something about holidays that brings out unrealistic expectations from cooks—and guests. We can't control what guests think, but we can control our own approach and attitude toward what we put on the table. First acknowledge what's actually doable, given the time and resources you have. Edit the menu as needed. Make what you can, buy what you can't. We've totally had celebration meals where our ambition got the better of us and a dish or two will end up not making it to the table. Truth be told, no one misses those dishes—especially if they don't expect them.

FUN FACT: The Mandarin characters for the names of Chinese restaurants often don't have direct translations in English. This is too bad, because a lot of restaurants have names that tell a story. For example, one of our local restaurants is called Spicy Style of Sichuan. But the Chinese name is 蜀一蜀二 (shu-yi shu-er). 蜀 or shu is the Three Kingdoms (circa 220–280 CE) Chinese name for the region surrounding what's now known as Sichuan. 蜀一蜀二 borrows from the homophonic phrase 數一數二, which means "ranked no. 1, no. 2." One clever character change takes us on a journey that's part history, part pride, part throw-down.

FAMILY-STYLE PORTIONS

The recipes in this book serve four as part of a family-style meal containing multiple dishes. If you're not making a feast and you're cooking a single recipe, such as Hoisin Beef with Snow Peas (page 79), it may serve two as a meal with rice. If you're making a weeknight dinner for four, you may need three dishes plus a soup. Though if you have big eaters, you'll want to bump up the portions.

LUNAR MONTHS	1	2	3	4	5	6	7	8	9	10	11	12	13	14	15
JAN	20	21	22	23	24	25	26	27	28	29	12TH LUNAR MONTH	2	3	4	5
FEB	22	23	24	25	26	27	28	29	30	1ST LUNAR MONTH	2	3	4	5	6
MAR	21	22	23	24	25	26	27	28	29	2ND LUNAR MONTH	2	3	4	5	6
APR	23	24	25	26	27	28	29	30	3RD LUNAR MONTH	2	3	4	5	6	7
MAY	23	24	25	26	27	28	29	4TH LUNAR MONTH	2	3	4	5	6	7	8
JUN	25	26	27	28	29	5TH LUNAR MONTH	2	3	4	5	6	7	8	9	10
JUL	26	27	28	29	31	6TH LUNAR MONTH	2	3	4	5	6	7	8	9	10
AUG	27	28	29	7TH LUNAR MONTH	2	3	4	5	6	7	8	9	10	11	12
SEP	29	30	8TH LUNAR MONTH	2	3	4	5	6	7	8	9	10	11	12	13
OCT	29	30	9TH LUNAR MONTH	2	3	4	5	6	7	8	9	10	11	12	13
NOV	10TH LUNAR MONTH	2	3	4	5	6	7	8	9	10	11	12	13	14	15
DEC	11TH LUNAR MONTH	2	3	4	5	6	7	8	9	10	11	12	13	14	15

16	17	18	19	20	21	22	23	24	25	26	27	28	29	30	31
6	7	8	9	10	11	12	13	14	15	16	17	18	19	20	21
7	8	9	10	11	12	13	14	15	16	17	18	19	20		
7	8	9	10	11	12	13	14	15	16	17	18	19	20	21	22
8	9	10	11	12	13	14	15	16	17	18	19	20	21	22	
9	10	11	12	13	14	15	16	17	18	19	20	21	22	23	24
11	12	13	14	15	16	17	18	19	20	21	22	23	24	25	
11	12	13	14	15	16	17	18	19	20	21	22	23	24	25	26
13	14	15	16	17	18	19	20	21	22	23	24	25	26	27	28
14	15	16	17	18	19	20	21	22	23	24	25	26	27	28	
14	15	16	17	18	19	20	21	22	23	24	25	26	27	28	29
16	17	18	19	20	21	22	23	24	25	26	27	28	29	30	
16	17	18	19	20	21	22	23	24	25	26	27	28	29	30	12TH LUNAR MONTH

RECIPE EFFORT RATINGS

How long a recipe takes to complete varies from person to person. To give some indication of time, each recipe includes a low, medium, or high rating on the amount of active effort it takes. Making dumplings from scratch, for example, is "high" because it takes more active effort and time than the few minutes it takes ("low") to stir-fry bok choy. While simmering chicken broth takes a couple of hours, the active time is less than 30 minutes, so that ranks as "low" effort. Here's the general guidance:

● ○ ○ **LOW** = 30 minutes or less of active effort

● ● ○ **MEDIUM** = 60 minutes or less of active effort

● ● ● **HIGH** = More than 60 minutes of active effort

BEVERAGES AND DESSERTS

It can be challenging to pair wines with Chinese food because a meal has so many different flavors. One approach is to match the wine with the predominant flavor or the featured dish. Working with the staff at the wine shop is a good way to home in on the right wine for your meal and budget. Beer tends to be easier to pair. Tsingtao beer is widely available in the United States and is a good bet. If you live in a city where there is a Chinese tea shop, you can ask the staff what tea might go best with your meal. Chinese teas can range from delicate and floral to hearty and fermented. Our family favorite is jasmine tea.

While we love desserts, we don't typically have them after a meal. Instead, we'll serve a platter of cut fruit—this is why many Chinese restaurants bring orange slices to close out the dinner. As it warrants, feel free to serve your favorite dessert. In major cities, there are many Asians bakeries that sell Asian-style (i.e., less sweet) cakes, tarts, and pastries. One of our favorites that we buy from a nearby Asian bakery is a light sponge cake filled with whipped cream and fresh strawberries.

Key Ingredients, Equipment, and Techniques

Many ingredients in our recipes should be available at a well-stocked grocery store. If you have access to an Asian market, you'll have more choices for key items, such as soy sauce, noodles, rice, and produce. Not all Asian markets are the same, however. For example, the national chain 99 Ranch Market is a good bet for Chinese or Taiwanese ingredients. We also have the regional chain of Asian Family Markets, where we regularly go to check out the selection of Chinese and Taiwanese soy sauces. H Mart, however, is Korean-centric and has fewer Chinese brands. It doesn't mean you shouldn't shop at H Mart, just that you may not find the range of Chinese ingredients that you would at 99 Ranch. If we ever want to do kalbi, H Mart is the place to get short ribs, kimchi and other banchan, and anything else we might need for Korean barbecue. In the Seattle area, we also have Uwajimaya, a local chain of Japanese-centric markets that has been around for ninety-five years. It has an extensive selection of Japanese products—and a gorgeous seafood counter—but not as many specialty Chinese ingredients. We go to Uwajimaya for the meats, including the thinly sliced cuts for hot pot; seafood, especially when we want to make sushi at home; and all the components for making dashi and miso soup. We tend to shop across a few different Asian markets to get the full range of foods we need—because we don't cook just Chinese meals.

Of course, there are many small, family-owned Asian markets out there. Support them if you can. There are now many online options to order Asian ingredients too. Umamicart.com offers a solid range of ingredients and delivers to your door. They were a lifesaver when we were visiting a small town that didn't have any Asian markets nearby. We ordered the ingredients we needed for cooking and everything arrived safely in a few days. Pearl River Mart in New York City has brick-and-mortar shops, but you can also buy select items—including food, clothing, dishes, and kitchenware—online at PearlRiver.com. If you do get to New York, definitely pop into one of the locations to explore. (At the SoHo location, we found a qipao-inspired crop top for Meilee that was perfect for acknowledging the traditional design but bringing it forward for a modern teenager.) For Sichuan pepper, TheMalaMarket.com and FlyByJing.com are two options. For condiments, especially chili crisp and soy sauce, FlyByJing.com and Yunhai.shop are great resources. If there's a particular brand of ingredient you need but can't find at a store near you, search for it online.

MOM SAYS: It takes time to build a well-stocked kitchen. Start by getting the ingredients you need for a given set of recipes. Over time, as you try new recipes, you will expand your collection of ingredients. The same goes for equipment. Start with essentials and add tools as you go. If you're just getting into Chinese cooking or maybe you've just moved into your first apartment, here's a "start-up pack" of items to consider. Some combination of these items would also make a great housewarming or registry gift.

- Bamboo steamer (10-inch)
- Bean thread (cellophane noodles)
- Chili sauce and/or chili crisp
- Chinese rolling pin (10- or 12-inch)
- Cornstarch
- Cutting board (18-inch or bigger, wood or plastic; *do not buy a glass cutting board*)
- Dried Chinese noodles
- Dried shiitake mushrooms
- Hoisin sauce
- Knife (8-inch chef's knife)
- Rice
- Rice vinegar
- Sesame oil
- Soup ladle
- Soy sauce
- Tongs (9- or 12-inch)
- White pepper powder
- Wok (14-inch, carbon steel)
- Wok spatula

KEY INGREDIENTS

Pantry

BEAN SAUCE AND SWEET BEAN SAUCE: Both are made with fermented soy beans and can be used in stir-fries or soups to enrich the flavor and add body. The difference is that sweet bean sauce contains flour, sugar, and salt.

BEAN THREAD: Also called cellophane, glass, or saifun noodles, bean thread is made of mung bean and potato starch. Don't confuse bean thread with rice vermicelli or rice sticks. For stir-fries or fillings, first soak the bean thread in room-temperature water for up to 30 minutes to soften. If adding to soup, there's no need to rehydrate; add the bean thread about 5 minutes before serving.

CHILI BEAN SAUCE/PASTE: Made from fermented chilies and fava beans (Pixian style) or soybeans, depending on where it originates. The spice level ranges from mild to incendiary. A good mass-market brand with several sauce options is Lee Kum Kee.

CHILI CRISP: This popular condiment usually contains chili, chili oil, garlic, and other mix-ins, such as onions, peanuts, and sesame seeds. Each brand has its own recipe. Add it to whatever food you choose.

CHILI SAUCE: Chili sauce (without soybeans) is commonly made with red chilies. Labels typically aren't specific about the type of chili, so be aware that any given jar might be mild or it might torch your palate. If you have chili bean sauce, you don't necessarily need to have chili sauce too. But it's fun to try a variety of condiments.

CHINESE RED DATES (JUJUBES): These dried dates can be eaten as is or added to broths. They are said to help balance your body's qi—or life force. Buy large, plump dried dates. If you can find fresh jujubes, try them; they taste like mini sweet apples.

CHINESE SAUSAGE: Dried or fresh sausages are usually made from pork and unrendered fat, and have a sweet flavor. It's commonly referred to by its Cantonese name "lap cheong." To cook, either steam them whole or slice and brown in a pan before eating or incorporating in other dishes.

DRIED BAMBOO LEAVES: These long, slender leaves are essential for making zongzi. Look for leaves that are intact and not brittle. Soak leaves in room-temperature water for at least 30 minutes to rehydrate.

DRIED LOTUS LEAVES: These massive leaves look like giant fans and are used to make the dim-sum favorite sticky rice in lotus leaf. The leaves are folded in half, with the khaki-colored underside of the leaves showing in the package. When buying, look for leaves that have an earthy-green color on the topside and avoid any that are dull and brittle. Soak leaves in room-temperature water for about 1 hour to rehydrate.

DRIED RED CHILIES: There are many different types of dried red chili peppers. Asian markets sell generic ones and the packaging may not reveal the specific variety of pepper. However, here are some examples of varieties that may be available: Japones, arbol, Tien Tsin (named after the city Tianjian), and Sichuan. You can throw some in a stir-fry as you're heating the oil or use them to make chili oil. You also can add as many pods as you think you can handle to a hot pot broth for an exciting evening.

DRIED SHIITAKE MUSHROOMS: Dried shiitake mushrooms vary in type, size, and grade.

The ones with the crackle-like pattern on the cap are called hua gu, which means "flower mushroom." These tend to cost more. The other, more utilitarian type of shiitake is called xiang gu, or "fragrant mushroom." The caps are thinner, darker, and smoother. For the purposes of the recipes in this book, a medium shiitake mushroom is one that has a cap measuring roughly 1½ to 2 inches in diameter. If you get bigger or smaller mushrooms, then adjust the amount accordingly.

To rehydrate: The soaking time can vary depending on the size of the mushrooms. Smaller ones take less time. Larger mushroom caps may take all day or overnight to fully rehydrate. For shiitake with 1- to 2-inch caps, allow for 2 to 3 hours of soaking time. You can speed up rehydration time by using hot or even boiling water. Turn the caps so the gills (underside) of the caps are in the water. The mushrooms will float at the surface of the water and reconstitute from the bottom up. If you have a small plate that fits inside the bowl, you can weigh down the mushrooms to submerge them fully in the water. This will help speed up the process.

The exception: When making a broth, such as Chinese-Style Chicken Broth (page 226), you can add dried shiitake directly to the water without soaking. By the time the broth is done simmering, the mushrooms will have fully rehydrated and added their essence to the flavor.

DRIED WOOD EAR MUSHROOMS: This crunchy, mildly flavored fungus is used for texture in any number of dishes and for its purported health benefits. There are many varieties and sizes of wood ear, which can make it confusing to buy—and to measure for a recipe. The larger ones, when rehydrated, must be cut. Smaller ones can be used whole. The cloud ear fungus is a type of wood ear, but it's typically grown at higher altitudes and is from the Yunnan region. The *yun* in Yunnan means "cloud." So *yun er* (云耳) is "cloud ear." *Mu er* (木耳) is "wood ear."

To rehydrate: Soak in warm water for 20 to 30 minutes, or until reconstituted. If whole, trim the stem end (the white stump-like knob) and cut into desired size. Pre-cut strips can be used right away.

FRIED GARLIC: Asian-style dried garlic granules can add quick flavor and texture sprinkled on a stir-fry. You can also add it to a sauce for some toasted garlicky flavor. Combine them with fried shallots for extra layers of flavor.

FRIED SHALLOTS: Also known as fried red onions, fried shallots are great to sprinkle on any number of dishes, including stir-fries and soups. Combine them with fried garlic for extra layers of flavor.

GOJI BERRIES: In traditional Chinese medicine (TCM), dried goji berries are thought to have many healing properties. Among them, goji detoxifies and also brings moisture that can help dry coughs. Pop some in a broth, a tea, or stir-fry.

HOISIN SAUCE: Made from yellow beans, sugar, vinegar, salt, and many other seasonings according to the manufacturer's recipe. It's often used as a condiment or mixed with other sauces to flavor stir-fries. Most people are

familiar with hoisin as a constant companion at pho restaurants. Garlic-flavored hoisin is available too.

NOODLES: There are numerous types of wheat noodles you can buy, both dried and fresh. Thin, medium, wide, shaved, knife-cut—everything you can imagine. Which you buy depends on preference. We tend to buy medium-width dried noodles as our multipurpose noodles. We sometimes buy fresh noodles, of which there are many styles.

OIL: Use a neutral, all-purpose oil such as vegetable or canola. You can use peanut or corn oil, being mindful of any allergies or sensitivities. Olive oil—especially extra-virgin olive oil—is too pungent. (Plus, you wouldn't want to subject a fine olive oil to the high heat of wok cooking, which would kill all the nuances in the flavor.)

PRESERVED CHINESE MUSTARD GREENS: This is a pickle that can go in soups and stir-fries or be used as a condiment or in a filling. Look for it in Asian markets in the refrigerated section. Sometimes, you'll find shelf-stable packages in a pantry aisle.

RICE: There are so many types and brands of rice. Usually, people like to eat the rice they grew up with. Our family keeps a few varieties in stock: medium-grain (Japanese-style rice), long-grain (jasmine), brown medium-grain (Japanese-style), and glutinous or sweet rice. For everyday rice, we typically make medium-grain. This is strictly personal preference. You can use whichever type of rice you like. Sweet rice is what goes into

FRIED GARLIC

DRIED
RED CHILIES

FRIED SHALLOTS

ROCK SUGAR

BEAN THREAD

WHEAT NOODLES

RICE VERMICELLI

zongzi or sticky rice in lotus leaf. In a pinch or for convenience, the Nishiki (or other similar brands) microwave rice packets are surprisingly good. See Washing and Cooking Rice (page 31).

RICE VERMICELLI: For dried rice noodles, look for what's called "rice vermicelli" or "rice stick." This is what goes in Rice Vermicelli with Vegetables (page 108). Soak in warm tap water for 20 to 30 minutes prior to using.

RICE VINEGAR: Rice vinegars are made from fermented glutinous rice. Look for unseasoned rice vinegar, such as the Marukan brand. If you like pungency, try a Chinese black vinegar, such as the ones from the Chinkiang region. Alternatively, for dips, you can use an everyday balsamic vinegar in place of the black vinegar.

ROCK SUGAR: Also called "rock candy," this is crystallized sugar made from liquid brown sugar. It comes in different forms, including large jagged chunks or smaller lumps that look like lozenges. Rock sugar adds sheen to the sauces for red-braised dishes. If you can't find rock sugar, use dark brown sugar instead.

SESAME OIL: Sesame oil is intended to be used as a finishing oil in a stir-fry or soup. It also adds great flavor to fillings, marinades, or dipping sauces. It's not meant to be used as a cooking oil, however. The oil can be made from white or black sesame seeds. Asian sesame oils tend to be made from toasted sesame seeds, which yield the amber color. If you don't use a lot of sesame oil, store in the refrigerator.

SICHUAN PEPPER: These reddish-brown peppercorns will cause a tingling and numbing sensation on your palate. Also called prickly ash, it's an essential ingredient in Sichuan cooking. There is no substitute for Sichuan peppercorn. If you can't get to an Asian market, visit a spice shop or the bulk spice section at your market, or you can buy them online from Mala Market at TheMalaMarket.com. Before using, toast the peppercorns in a dry skillet over medium heat for 3 to 4 minutes, stirring frequently. Then grind to your preferred coarseness.

SOY SAUCE: Soy sauce is *the* essential ingredient. You can get a good soy sauce starting at about $4 or $5. Keep in mind that there's a whole world of soy sauces beyond the mass-market brands like Kikkoman. Soy sauce is unique to its cuisine of origin. A Japanese soy sauce that a sushi chef might serve with fine sashimi is not the same as a Chinese soy sauce that you'd subject to the high heat of a stir-fry. Ideally, you should get a Chinese soy sauce. Check the label and make sure it says "naturally fermented and brewed" so you know they took the time to make the soy sauce properly. If the ingredients include hydrolyzed soy protein, then choose another option. Such a soy sauce won't have the depth of flavor like one that's been naturally fermented and brewed. Within Chinese soy sauces, you will find designations for light, dark, thick, paste, aged. Light soy sauce does not refer to the calorie count; it refers to the color and viscosity. Light soy sauce tends to be saltier. The darker or thicker sauces usually are used for braises and are less salty. Aged soy sauces have an intense flavor that may be an acquired taste. One "all-purpose" soy sauce that's great for any of the recipes in this book is the yellow-label Kimlan.

MOM SAYS: If you have either of my first two books, *Chinese Soul Food* or *Vegetarian Chinese Soul Food*, please check out the sections on soy sauce. I encourage everyone to try different soy sauces because they all taste so different and have different levels of salinity. You don't eat one kind of candy or ice cream, so don't restrict yourself to one kind of soy sauce. Asian markets and online shops have more and more options these days.

STAR ANISE: This has a licorice flavor and is a key component in many "red braise" dishes, such as red-braised beef noodle soup or red-braised pork belly. Use sparingly because the flavor can easily overpower a dish.

WHITE PEPPER POWDER: White pepper is aged and fermented, which gives it a floral, nuanced heat. It is generally not interchangeable with black pepper. While you can buy white peppercorns and grind them yourself, it's more convenient to buy a small bottle of white pepper powder from an Asian market. You want the white pepper to lightly dust the surface of the food. You don't want to see specks of pepper.

Fresh Items

DUMPLING WRAPPERS: Also called potsticker wrappers or gyoza wrappers, these round wrappers are used for making boiled, steamed, or pan-fried dumplings. In Asian markets, you can find dumpling wrappers in different thicknesses for each type of preparation. The thicker the wrapper, the hardier it is and more able to withstand frying or boiling.

EGG ROLL WRAPPERS: Egg roll wrappers are flour-based and are 7- to 8-inches square. They're widely available in supermarkets. Use them within several days of purchase or freeze them and defrost as needed.

RICE CAKE: Rice cake comes in slices, batons, and balls. They can be used in soups and stir-fries. Look for them in the refrigerated section. They sometimes are frozen or dried. Since they're vacuum-sealed, they'll keep in the refrigerator for a long time. This is a key ingredient in Korean cooking, so if you want the widest selection of types of rice cake, visit a Korean market, such as H Mart.

SPRING ROLL WRAPPERS: These square, crepe-like wrappers are used for making the delicately crispy spring rolls. They're 7- to 8-inches square and are sold frozen. Don't confuse these with the Vietnamese-style round spring roll wrappers, which are dried. Wei-Chuan or Spring Home brands are widely available. Defrost overnight in the refrigerator before using.

TOFU: Tofu is made from soy-milk curds that are pressed into blocks of different firmness: silken, soft, medium, firm, extra-firm. Tofu is versatile and appears in every form in every type of dish, from appetizers to desserts. For recipes in this book, use Chinese-style soft or medium-firm tofu. You can use Japanese silken or Korean soondubu if you'd like, with the caveat that they are delicate and not intended to hold a cube shape.

SPICED TOFU: This is pressed tofu that's braised in a soy sauce–based liquid with five-spice powder. It's then baked until the surface is dry. The tofu can be sliced to use in stir-fries or a salad.

WONTON WRAPPERS: Wonton wrappers are flour-based and widely available in supermarkets. If you can get to a Chinese market, you will be able to find wonton wrappers of different thicknesses. Where a thin wrapper might be used for wonton soup, a thicker wrapper might be used for fried wontons. Use them within several days of purchase or freeze and defrost as needed.

Key Vegetables

BABY BOK CHOY: Also called Shanghai bok choy, these jade-colored cabbages are widely available, even in non-Asian markets. Look for small-to-medium heads (4 to 6 inches long) for the most tender leaves. Some Asian markets sell bok choy mui, which are extra-small bok choy that are 3 to 4 inches long. In non-Asian markets, the baby bok choy may be overgrown and can be 12 inches long or so. The more overgrown they are, the less tender. That said, use what's available to you. There are different varieties of baby bok choy: the white bok choy with dimpled dark-green leaves are hardier and may need a slightly longer cooking time.

To trim: Slice about ¼ inch off the core end, where there sometimes is a tiny stump. Then snap each leaf stem as close to the core as you can. Proceed with rinsing. Alternatively, slice the head of bok choy in half lengthwise. Then make angled cuts on each side of the core and remove.

This will release the leaves so you can wash them. If you don't remove the core, dirt can get trapped inside. Some folks like to cook smaller baby bok choy whole, which looks pretty but is hard to eat.

BEAN SPROUTS: Bean sprouts add good crunch to stir-fries and fillings. When buying bean sprouts, get the freshest-looking ones and check the sell-by date. If there is any sign of slime at the bottom of the package or the sprouts look brown from bruising, don't buy them. Once you buy bean sprouts, use them within a day or two. They don't hold well. The Chinese typically add bean sprouts to cooked dishes, including soups, stir-fries, and fillings.

CHINESE BROCCOLI (GAI LAN): Chinese broccoli, or gai lan, has dark-green leaves and long stalks. You can slice the stalks thinly and cook with the leaves. If you go to an Asian market, you will also find baby gai lan (called gai lan mui). These are more tender and worth the effort to seek out the next time you go to an Asian market.

To trim: Cut about ½ inch off the bottom of the stalks. You can leave the stalk whole, which makes them hard to eat without a fork and knife. Or you can slice the stalk thinly and roughly chop the leaves.

CHINESE CABBAGE/NAPA CABBAGE: Chinese cabbage, also called napa cabbage, is a versatile ingredient that can just as easily be a filler ingredient as a star. Mildly sweet, Chinese cabbage can be stir-fried, steamed, added to soups and fillings, and even used as the liner for

BABY BOK CHOY,
A.K.A. SHANGHAI
BOK CHOY

CHINESE CABBAGE,
A.K.A. NAPA CABBAGE

a steamer basket full of dumplings. A head of Chinese cabbage sometimes can be quite large, but it will store in the produce bin for a long time. In some Asian markets, you can find Wa Wa cabbage—or "doll" Chinese cabbage. These are small heads of cabbage and tend to be packaged in bulk. If you find them in the store, give them a try. The flavor is delicate and sweet.

To trim: Peel off any outer leaves that are damaged or wilting. Cut the cabbage in half lengthwise and then cut each half into quarters. Cut the wedge of core off, use the leaves you need, and store the rest.

CHINESE CELERY: Chinese celery has long, slender ribs and a pungent flavor. They're sold in clusters. For any recipe that calls for celery, you can use Chinese celery, if you prefer. It is a staple you should keep in the refrigerator.

CHINESE CHIVES: Chinese chives have long, flat leaves and are so pungent they'll take over your refrigerator. Trim the root end and any wilted leaves. Chop the rest to use in dumpling fillings or stir-fries. They taste great in scrambled eggs too.

CHINESE EGGPLANT: Chinese and Japanese eggplants are long and thin and dark to bright purple in color. Rinse before using, but you don't have to peel the skin.

To trim: Cut off the green stem. You can then cut them into batons, rounds, or wedges depending on your preference or per recipe instructions. You also can steam them whole, slice open, and top with your preferred seasoning.

CHINESE MUSTARD GREENS (GAI CHOY): Chinese mustard greens, or gai choy, have a bright but pungent flavor. The larger heads have bulbous stems and unwieldy leaves. Smaller heads, often sold in multiples, are more delicate. Look for the small mustard greens in Chinese markets, where they're often labeled "xue li hong."

To trim: Cut about ¼ to ½ inch off the core end. Then snap apart the leaves, which sometimes can be unwieldy. Rinse thoroughly in cool water before using.

CILANTRO: Cilantro is called xiang cai, or "fragrant vegetable." This herb shows up as a finishing touch in many cold and hot dishes. It adds its namesake fragrance to balance heavy flavors. It's a key accent in the Dumpling Dipping Sauce (page 58) and West Lake Beef Soup (page 118).

To trim: Wash thoroughly. If the roots are still intact, you can mince and use them, but many people discard the roots. Use the leaves and the stems, which can be minced.

DAIKON: Daikon radish can be pickled, braised, stir-fried, steamed, or cooked in soup. Daikon tend to be long and lean and are often sold next to Korean radish, which is rounder and squatter, with a halo of green skin. While daikon is known to be milder, both types of radish will work in recipes.

To trim: Cut off the top and tail and peel like you would a carrot.

幸
福
饗
宴

EDAMAME: The Chinese call edamame mao dou, or "fuzzy bean." The shelled beans can be stir-fried or steamed. Look for shelled frozen edamame. You also can buy frozen edamame pods, but you will have to defrost them and remove the shell before cooking. Try the Stir-Fried Edamame with Shrimp (page 112).

GARLIC: Look for bulbs of garlic that have bright skins and firm cloves. Avoid ones that have brown spots, feel soft, or have green sprouts in the middle. For many recipes in this book, you can finely mince, crush, or smash the garlic as specified. It's hard to beat the flavor of fresh garlic, but you can also use jarred minced garlic for convenience. Asian-style dried garlic, which comes in small packets, is also a great way to add flavor and crunch to a dish. Sprinkle some on the dish as a finishing touch.

GINGER: Ginger adds warmth and spice, but it also counterbalances any off-flavors and brightens a dish. When buying, look for a succulent piece that has bright skin. If the skin is dull and wrinkly, skip it. If the piece is too large, break off the chunk that you need. The general rules for ginger in this book: There is no need to peel the ginger when the recipe calls for slices. Peel the ginger if the recipe calls for grated or minced ginger. You can freeze ginger if you happen to buy too big a piece and know you can't use it all in a reasonable amount of time. Let it defrost before using.

GREEN ONIONS: Also known as scallions, green onions often are combined with ginger and garlic to increase the pungency of dishes. For

the recipes in this book, use both the white and green parts of the stalk.

To trim: Cut off the root end. If any of the greens have any brown edges, trim them off. You can save the roots and put them in water to regenerate. If the green onions happen to sit in the refrigerator a little too long and start to wilt or brown, trim off the root, then peel off the outer layer. Chances are the inner stalk is still perfectly usable.

MUSHROOMS (FRESH): While shiitake mushrooms are a go-to for us, the variety of fresh mushrooms that are now available in supermarkets keeps growing. White or brown beech mushrooms, oyster mushrooms, baby king oyster, maitake, and enoki are just some of the mushrooms you can find. Feel free to experiment with different varieties. Also, if all you can get are brown or cremini mushrooms, use those.

SNOW PEAS: Snow peas appear in recipes as much for a pop of color as for texture and flavor. Select bright-green snow peas that don't have brown spots or wrinkled skin.

To trim: Snap off the stem before using.

SUGAR SNAP PEAS: The sweet, delicate flavor of sugar snaps brightens stir-fries. Trim off the stem before using.

SWEET POTATO: There are different types of sweet potatoes, which often are confused with yams. For the Sweet Potato Fritters recipe (page 151), red garnet sweet potatoes are ideal. Scrub clean

WHOLE GINGER

WHOLE GARLIC CLOVES

SLICED
GINGER

CHOPPED GARLIC

SMASHED
GARLIC

JULIENNED
GINGER

MINCED GINGER

CRUSHED GARLIC

GRATED GINGER

before peeling and prepping as instructed. A great shortcut is to use frozen sweet potatoes. Follow the directions on the package to cook.

TAIWANESE CABBAGE: A head of Taiwanese cabbage looks like a supersized, flattened green cabbage. These have a mildly sweet flavor and don't need much more than a few minutes in a hot wok with a dash of soy sauce. When buying, look for the smallest head you think you could reasonably consume in a few weeks. Asian markets often cut the larger cabbages into halves.

To trim: Remove any damaged outer leaves. Cut out the hard inner core.

WINTER MELON: This gourd can be round or oblong like watermelon. The flesh is white with thick seeds, and the rind can be dark green or light green with creamy striations. When cooked or candied, the flesh becomes translucent. Winter melon is typically sold in chunks.

To trim: Scrape out the seeds and, using a knife, carefully shave off the rind before cooking. The rind can be quite hard, so be careful.

YU CHOY: Yu choy is great for stir-fries. It's also known as rapeseed, which is the plant from which canola oil is derived. Look for a bunch with unbruised leaves. Asian markets sell yu choy mui—baby yu choy—which is more tender than the mature ones.

To trim: Cut about ½ inch off the end. The rest of the stem and the leaves can be sliced or roughly chopped.

EQUIPMENT

CHOPSTICKS: Chopsticks are multipurpose and can be used for cooking, eating, and serving. In the kitchen, a pair of cooking chopsticks can beat eggs, mix fillings, handle frying foods, and do what tongs can do for arranging or picking up foods. Everyday bamboo chopsticks are great. Cooking chopsticks are about 15 inches long. The extra length makes it easier to handle ingredients that are still in the active stages of cooking. Chopstick styles do differ from culture to culture. Where Japanese chopsticks tend to taper to a point, for example, Chinese chopsticks tend to be thicker and have a blunt, round tip.

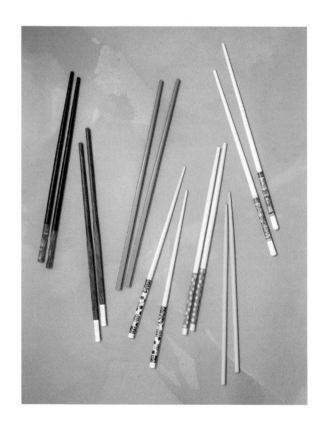

CHEF'S KNIFE: An 8-inch chef's knife can handle most tasks. You don't have to spend a lot on a starter knife. An OXO knife, for example, will cost you less than $20. But if you're a serious cook, invest in a knife. What brand you buy is a personal choice that depends on budget and how a knife feels in your hand. Visit a reputable knife shop or kitchenware shop to try different knives.

CLEAVER: A cleaver is the most traditional knife in a Chinese kitchen. It can do everything: slice, chop, smash, crack, scrape, scoop, and more. All Asian markets sell inexpensive cleavers for $20 to $30. A Dexter Chinese cleaver—which is popular among Chinese restaurant chefs—will cost around $40 to $50.

CUTTING BOARD: Wood or plastic cutting boards—not glass—are your best bet. For wood boards, go for a softer material such as walnut or maple. This protects your knife. Plastic cutting boards are durable and can go in the dishwasher. Get a board that's at least 17 or 18 inches wide. If you have the counter space, you can get a larger butcher-block-style board, such as the ones from Boos. Ideally, you'll have a second cutting board so that you can designate one for produce and the other for proteins.

FAT SKIMMER: This is a fine-mesh tool with an upright handle that is great for skimming the scum off the surface of broths or braises, or the debris from deep-frying. Look for these online, at a kitchenware shop, or at Asian markets.

FINE-MESH SIEVES (STRAINER): Fine-mesh sieves are useful for straining broths or sauces that contain loose aromatics or ingredients that require soaking.

LADLE: A ladle is an essential tool for dishing out broths, soups, and other liquids.

MEASURING CUPS AND SPOONS: Standard measuring cups and spoons are essential. Also consider getting mini angled measuring cups, such as the OXO 4-tablespoon measuring cup, which is helpful for portioning soy sauce and other liquid ingredients.

METAL WORK BOWLS: Keep a stack of lightweight stainless-steel work bowls in several sizes. They're durable, convenient, and essential for containing all the prepped ingredients. You can also put them in the dishwasher.

RICE COOKER: You don't have to have a rice cooker, but it sure makes life easier. Cooking rice on the stove is straightforward, and some people prefer it. But we can't imagine being without a rice cooker. Rice cookers range in cost from $20 for a tiny one to $500 for a bells-and-whistles model, but you can get a solid cooker for about $60 to $70. High-end computerized rice cookers are programmable and adjust the soaking, cooking, and steaming times according to the type of rice.

ROLLING PIN: Chinese rolling pins are dowel-style pins that are usually 10 to 12 inches long and about ¾ inch in diameter. Depending on the type of wood, a rolling pin will cost from $2 to $10. This is a necessary tool for making dumplings from scratch. You can also use these for scallion pancakes and other dough-based recipes.

SAUCE DISHES: Small ceramic sauce dishes are not only useful for dipping sauces but are also handy for holding the spices and aromatics that will go into a recipe. Any kitchenware shop sells them. You can also find an inexpensive dish selection at Daiso.

SCALE: Get a digital scale that can switch between US and metric. Using weight is a much more accurate way to measure ingredients.

STEAMER: Steamers are available in bamboo, stainless steel, and aluminum. You can find an assortment of dedicated steamer pots at any Asian market or online. Bamboo is ideal because it's absorbent and prevents condensation. With metal or glass steamer lids, the condensation drips back down onto your food, leaving water spots. If you have beautiful dumplings, you don't want water spots. When buying, choose a three-piece 10-inch bamboo steamer set plus an 11-inch steaming ring that will allow you to convert a Dutch oven or stockpot into a steamer system.

STEAMER AND HOT PLATE GRIPPER/TONGS: These special gripper tongs are for lifting hot dishes out of a steamer. If you plan on doing a lot of steaming, these special grippers are helpful.

STEAMER PAPER: These are made of parchment or a food-safe synthetic material. They are pre-cut to fit a 10-inch steamer and help prevent sticking.

STRAINER/SPIDER: A spider is useful for straining and lifting foods out of hot oil or boiling water. There are many styles of spiders. You can get a traditional wire and bamboo version or a stainless-steel version.

TONGS: Short and long tongs are useful for any number of cooking tasks. If you have space to have multiple, get several in different sizes. Make sure to get ones with spring action and a padded handle.

WOK: Woks are superheroes in the kitchen because they can handle high-heat stir-fries, steaming, deep-frying, braising, simmering, smoking, and more. Traditionally, woks have a round bottom, which helps to concentrate heat. But round-bottom woks require a gas stove, and many people have electric or flat-top ranges. The solution is to get a flat-bottomed wok. Here's what you need: a 14-inch carbon-steel flat-bottom wok with a wood handle. Carbon steel is key because it heats and cools quickly, is relatively light, and builds a patina over time—as long as you use and take care of the wok. Don't get stainless steel—it's too heavy and difficult to control. A trustworthy and affordable wok is the Joyce Chen 14-inch carbon-steel flat-bottom wok. It sells for under $40 and comes with a lid. While you can spend up to $100 or more on a wok, you truly don't need to. Look for the Joyce Chen wok online. If you go to an Asian market, you will find a good selection of carbon-steel woks. They may not be made by recognizable brands, but that doesn't matter.

WOK SPATULA: A wok spatula has a long handle and a wide, thin blade that helps you scoop and toss ingredients in a wok. A spatula with a thin metal blade works better than bamboo or plastic. Look for wok spatulas online or at an Asian market. You shouldn't spend more than $10 to $15.

PRESERVING WOK TRADITIONS

HOW TO SEASON A WOK: For a new wok, scrub it with soap and hot tap water to rid the surface of the factory finish. Dry with a towel. Set the wok on the stove and turn the heat to high. The heat helps to dry the wok completely. When the wok is really hot, there will be tiny wisps of smoke.

Next, coat the hot wok with oil: Starting from about 2 inches below the rim, slowly and in a swirling motion pour 3 tablespoons of vegetable oil down the side of the wok. Turn the heat to low. Add 1 bunch of green onions that have been cut into 3-inch segments and ½ cup of sliced ginger coins (¼ inch thick). It will sizzle a bit.

Now, using your wok spatula, stir and toss the green onions and ginger together. Then, using the combination like a sponge, push it up and down the sides of the wok to help coat the surface with oil. Do this for 2 to 3 minutes. Turn off the heat, discard the onions and ginger. Wipe the wok with a wad of paper towel to absorb any excess oil. Let cool. The wok is ready to go. Over time, especially if you use the wok to fry, the oil will help to develop the patina in the wok.

WOK MAINTENANCE: Treat a wok like a cast-iron pan. After the initial seasoning of the wok, don't use soap to wash it after use. Rinse immediately in warm water after use and give it a gentle scrub with a sponge. Dry thoroughly to prevent rusting: put it back on the stove to heat for about 1 minute to dry. If you do get some rust, scrub it with steel wool and reseason. The best practice for taking care of your wok is to cook from it often. If you don't use it, it will look splotchy and it won't develop a beautiful, rich patina.

Mom Says

Years ago, I asked friends who were traveling to Shanghai to bring back two Cen woks for me. I learned about the Cen brothers through my friend Grace Young, a cookbook author and advocate, who shared the beauty of these hand-hammered woks and explained how the pounding technique reinforces the structure and quality of the woks. (Sadly, due to gentrification in Shanghai, the brothers no longer operate their business.) I've been cooking from one of the woks, building the patina over time, and saved the other for this moment. As a milestone, Meilee received the wok and we seasoned it together. We call this process "opening" the wok. Now, we can cook from Meilee's wok to help build its patina. The wok that I've been using to cook for the family these past years eventually will go to Shen.

幸
福
饗
宴

TECHNIQUES

If a cook makes a technique look easy, it's because they've done it hundreds or thousands of times. Repetition builds muscle memory and, over time, reveals the secrets of ingredients and how they behave. Repetition teaches you how to make big or nuanced adjustments in how you handle tools or set up your kitchen workflow or manage time. And then, at some point, you'll feel at ease in the kitchen and project that well-earned confidence. It takes time, so give yourself room to learn and grow more proficient. Even experienced cooks can't claim to be experts at all cuisines. We each know what we know. The rest is discovery and practice.

Set Yourself Up for Success

There are a few practices that will help you have a great experience in the kitchen, especially if you're preparing a celebration dinner.

PLAN THE MENU: Decide what your menu will be. Make a list of recipes. This could take several days or several weeks.

READ THE RECIPES: Reading a recipe first helps you understand how much time you'll need for it, the ingredients you need, and whether there are any sub-recipes you need to make. You don't want to be caught in the moment trying to make a dish that requires, for example, an overnight marination period. If you're making a feast, knowing the timing of each recipe will help you create a prep schedule.

CLEAN YOUR WORKSPACE: Having an uncluttered work area in your kitchen will help you stay organized, especially as you're juggling multiple recipes.

Mom says: I start by wiping down all the counters and then sweeping the floor. It helps me with a mental transition from whatever I was doing before to meal-prep mode. Plus, having a clean workspace is important for hygiene and food safety.

MISE EN PLACE: This French term for "put everything in place" describes the practice of having all your ingredients ready to go. Measure seasonings, prepare all the ingredients (e.g., cut vegetables and proteins), get your tools ready, choose the serving platter. Group ingredients together so you can reach for them easily. This is essential when you're making stir-fries, because stir-frying happens quickly over high heat. If your ingredients aren't ready to add in the prescribed sequence, you risk overheating the oil or burning your food.

GIVE YOURSELF PLENTY OF TIME: Experienced cooks can "whip up something" because they have go-to recipes or techniques, shortcuts, and/or they know how to improvise based on whatever ingredients are available. If you're still learning the ways of the kitchen and especially for a celebration meal, you want to have plenty of time to plan and cook. So it's up to you to make sure you have that space to work through multiple recipes. Or enlist help! You don't have to make a feast all by yourself.

Washing and Cooking Rice

Before you cook white rice, it's a good idea to rinse it three or four times to remove extra starch and any dust or debris. If you have a large fine-mesh strainer, use that. What we typically do is place the rice in the rice cooker bowl. Add cool water to cover the rice and, using a hand or a rice paddle, quickly stir or agitate the rice for a few seconds. Then drain the water and repeat several times until the water is no longer cloudy. Is it the end of the world if you don't wash the rice? No, it's not. But we prefer the lighter texture of washed rice. Not all rice in all cuisines requires washing. For example, if you're making Italian risotto with carnaroli rice, you want to keep the starch to help thicken the dish. So prepare rice according to what you're making. For making steamed white rice for recipes in this book, we recommend washing.

To cook rice, we use a Zojirushi induction rice cooker. Add the amount of rice and water per the rice cooker recommendation, press a button, and the machine does the rest. If you don't have a rice cooker, you can make rice on the stove.

■ Put the rice in a large fine-mesh strainer. Rinse the rice for about 1 minute under cool running water. Alternatively, you can put the rice in a large bowl, cover with water, and run your hand or a rice paddle or wooden spoon through the rice a few times. Then pour out the water without spilling the rice and repeat the process several times until the water is no longer cloudy.

■ Put the rice in a 2-quart pot with a heavy bottom. Add 2½ cups of water. Make sure the rice is evenly spread out in the pot. Cover the pot with a lid. (If you want to soak the rice, add 30 minutes to your prep time. Let the rice soak in the pot for 30 minutes before cooking. Soaking the rice helps the heat penetrate the grains more easily.) Bring to a boil over medium heat, which should take 3 to 5 minutes. Reduce the heat to low. Cock the lid slightly to let the steam escape as the rice cooks. Cook for 25 to 30 minutes, or until all the water has been absorbed and the rice is no longer soggy. Remove the pot from the heat and let the rice rest in the pot, covered, for 10 to 15 minutes to let the rice finish steaming.

STEAMED RICE

MAKES 4 CUPS RICE

2 cups medium- or long-grain white rice

2½ cups water

SLICE

CHOP

ROLL CUT

JULIENNE

DICE

BIAS CUT

SMASH

MINCE

主
要
食
材
、
廚
具
、
廚
藝

Ways to Cut Vegetables

- Slice
- Dice
- Chop
- Mince

- Roll cut
- Bias cut
- Julienne
- Smash

Ways to Cut Proteins

There certainly are more types of proteins than are listed here. This is a cross section of common proteins. Use these preparation tips and apply them to your protein of choice.

CHICKEN: The most economical way to buy chicken is to get a whole bird and then break it down into pieces yourself. Understandably, that's not convenient or feasible for everyone. Just know that the more work the butcher does, the more that piece of meat costs. For example, boneless and skinless chicken breast can be double or triple the price per pound of a whole chicken. One of our neighborhood supermarkets sells whole chickens on sale for 99 cents per pound. The same brand of boneless, skinless chicken breasts sell for $6.99 per pound. That's a significant cost difference. We always buy chickens whole and butcher them ourselves into parts. The breasts and thighs go into stir-fries. The wings, carcass, bones, and drumsticks go into broth.

For stir-fries, you can cut chicken breast or thighs into cubes or large dice, or you can cut them into slivers. The benefit of smaller pieces is that they cook faster. The size of any single piece of chicken can vary. But here are some basic instructions for how to cut slivers:

Cut an 8-ounce chicken breast lengthwise into two to three strips, about 1½ inches wide, or about the size of chicken tenders. Then slice each strip of chicken crosswise into slivers. The exact size of the slivers is not as important as keeping the pieces relatively uniform. Similarly, you can cut chicken thighs into slivers.

To marinate: In a small bowl, combine the chicken with 1 tablespoon soy sauce and mix well. Add 2 teaspoons cornstarch and mix well again.

To parcook the chicken: Preheat a wok over high heat until wisps of smoke rise from the surface. Add 2 tablespoons vegetable oil and heat until it shimmers. Add the chicken and, using a spatula, quickly spread it into a single layer in the bowl of the wok. After about 15 seconds, stir-fry the chicken for about 1 more minute, or until the chicken is nearly cooked through. Remove the wok from the heat, transfer the chicken into a small bowl, and set aside. Now follow the instructions in the recipe you're making for combining this chicken with vegetables or other ingredients.

BEEF: We tend to use flank steak for our stir-fries. It's not an inexpensive cut, but it yields consistent results. There are many other types of cuts of beef. Your best bet is to use a cut that has marbling (fat), which has better flavor. Markets often package trim pieces as "stir-fry" meat. The drawback of these stir-fry packs is that you don't know what cuts they contain. It's usually a mix of trim from different cuts. The pieces can be large, so do slice them thinner against the grain, which will help with tenderness.

To cut flank steak: Trim any large pieces of membrane from an 8-ounce flank steak. Cut the flank in half or thirds lengthwise, or with the grain. Depending on the total width of the flank, you may get two or three sections that are about 3 inches wide. Cut these sections against the grain into ⅛-inch slices.

To marinate: Place the beef in a medium bowl. Add 1 tablespoon soy sauce and mix well. Add 2 teaspoons cornstarch and mix well again.

To parcook: Preheat a wok over high heat until wisps of smoke rise from the surface. Add 2 tablespoons vegetable oil and heat until it starts to shimmer. Gently add the beef and, using a spatula, quickly spread it into a single layer in the bowl of the wok. Sear the beef for about 15 seconds and then stir-fry for 1 to 2 minutes, breaking up any pieces that have stuck together. Remove the wok from the heat, transfer the beef to a medium bowl, and set aside. Now follow the instructions in the recipe you're making for combining this beef with vegetables or other ingredients.

PORK: For stir-fries, thin-cut pork chops work well. For braises, pork shoulder is your best bet. Of course, pork ribs are winners, especially in the Sweet-and-Sour Baby Back Ribs recipe (page 183).

To cut pork chops for stir-fry: Trim the fat off an 8-ounce thin-cut pork loin chop. Cut the chop lengthwise into two to three strips, about 1 inch wide, or about the size of chicken tenders. Then slice each strip of pork crosswise into slivers. The exact size of the slivers is not as important as keeping the pieces relatively uniform.

To marinate: In a small bowl, combine the pork with 1 tablespoon soy sauce and mix well. Add 2 teaspoons cornstarch and mix well again.

To parcook: Preheat a wok over high heat until wisps of smoke rise from the surface. Add 2 tablespoons vegetable oil and heat until it shimmers. Add the pork and, using a wok spatula, quickly spread it into a single layer in the bowl of the wok. After about 15 seconds, stir-fry the pork for about 1 more minute, or until the pork is nearly cooked through. Remove the wok from the heat, transfer the pork into a small bowl, and set aside. Now follow the instructions in the recipe you're making for combining this pork with vegetables or other ingredients.

SHRIMP: Traditionally, Chinese cooking uses shrimp in the shell and, ideally, you would buy the shrimp live. Then you know it's fresh! If you're into buying and preparing live shrimp, go for it. In the Pacific Northwest, where we live, we look forward to spot prawn season. These are sweet and delicious and are usually sold live. For the shrimp recipes in this book, feel free to use the shrimp that you have access to. That likely means frozen or previously frozen shrimp. If you can, look for wild shelled (i.e., peeled) shrimp. It's up to you what size shrimp you use. Medium shrimp are labeled 41/50, which means there are 41 to 50 shrimp per pound. Large shrimp are labeled 31/40; jumbo is roughly 26/30. (These are approximate.) Some shrimp are sold as peeled and deveined, which is the most convenient. Otherwise, you have to devein the shrimp yourself, which is a necessary step to clean out that digestive tract.

To prepare shrimp: Peel and devein about 8 ounces shrimp. Use a paring knife to cut into the back of the shrimp; start from the thick end and make a shallow cut down the length of the shrimp. You should be able to see the thin black line (which is the gunk you want to remove). Use the tip of the paring knife to remove the vein.

To marinate: In a small bowl, combine the deveined shrimp with 1 tablespoon soy sauce and mix well. Add 2 teaspoons cornstarch and mix well again. Set aside.

To parcook: Preheat a wok over high heat until wisps of smoke rise from the surface. Add 2 tablespoons vegetable oil and heat until it starts to shimmer. Add the shrimp in a single layer to the bowl of the wok and sear for 30 to 40 seconds, or until the shrimp have begun to turn pink. Flip the shrimp and sear for 30 to 40 seconds more. Remove the pan from the heat, transfer the shrimp to a small bowl, and set aside. Now follow the instructions in the recipe you're making for combining this shrimp with vegetables or other ingredients.

Stir-Frying 101

Once you learn the basics of stir-frying, you can mix any combination of vegetables, proteins, seasonings, and other ingredients to make a dish. Put on a pot of rice and you have a meal!

PREP: Cut all the crunchy vegetables into similar shapes or sizes. For any leafy greens, such as baby bok choy or Chinese cabbage, slice thin or into sections that are about 1 inch wide.

Prepare any aromatics you might be using, such as green onions, ginger, garlic, and such.

Measure the sauces you're using, such as soy sauce and hoisin sauce.

If you're using meats, cut into desired pieces and marinate. Then parcook: Preheat the wok over high heat until wisps of smoke rise from the surface. Add 2 tablespoons vegetable oil and let heat for a few seconds until the oil shimmers. Add the protein and spread into a single layer. Let sear for 30 to 60 seconds. Then, using the wok spatula, stir-fry for up to 1 minute. Remove from the heat, transfer the protein to a bowl, and set aside.

If you're using tofu, cut into desired pieces. If you're stir-frying tofu with other ingredients, be sure to use a firm tofu so that it holds up in the wok. If you're making a tofu dish and it's going to simmer in a broth or sauce, then you can use a soft or medium-firm tofu.

COOK: Rinse and dry the wok after you've parcooked the protein.

Return the wok to high heat. Add 1 teaspoon vegetable oil and immediately add any aromatics to let them heat up with the oil for a few seconds. Don't let the aromatics burn; the oil will heat quickly.

Quickly add the crunchy vegetables and stir-fry to combine. After the crunchy vegetables have had about a minute or so in the wok, add the softer, leafy vegetables. Stir to combine. Add the protein and stir-fry. Add the sauce(s) and stir to combine. If appropriate and desired, add a drizzle of sesame oil at the end to finish. Transfer to a plate.

AFTERCARE: Wash the wok as soon as you can. You can let it cool and wash it after you eat, but don't leave it longer than that. Wash the wok with warm water and a scrubby sponge but no soap.

Dry the wok thoroughly. If you have a well-developed patina, you can use a towel to dry off the surface water and then let it fully air-dry before storing. If you have a new wok, dry off the surface water with a towel, then set the wok on the stove over high heat for up to a minute to fully dry. This will help prevent rusting. Let the wok cool before storing.

Deep-Frying 101

If you have a deep fryer, great! That makes deep-frying so much simpler. Even though we have a deep fryer, it's not always set up. Usually, the amount of food we need to fry isn't worth the amount of oil necessary to fill the fryer. So we tend to deep-fry on the stove.

You can always use a wok for deep-frying. We find that we want to use the wok for stir-frying while we deep-fry other foods, so we reserve the wok for stir-fries and set up a separate Dutch oven for frying. That way we can have multiple dishes happening at the same time. Our go-to pot is a 4-quart Dutch oven. Use what you have available as long as it has deep sides.

We use canola oil as our all-purpose cooking oil. You certainly can use other neutral-flavored oils, such as vegetable oil, corn oil, and grapeseed. Peanut oil is fine to use if you don't have allergies.

ADD THE OIL: Add enough oil to the pot so that it can accommodate the height or thickness of your food. For example, if you're frying spring rolls, you will need to add enough oil to reach about 2 inches of depth. The total amount of oil will vary according to the diameter of your pot. If you have a pot that's 9 inches in diameter, you will need more oil to reach 2 inches of depth than if you had a pot that's 8 inches in diameter.

GET A THERMOMETER: It's essential to have a thermometer. The classic version is a candy thermometer that you can clip to the side of the pot. You want to be able to monitor the temperature and make sure that you adjust the heat as needed to maintain a consistent temperature. If you have the budget, get an infrared thermometer. You point it at the oil and it gives you a digital readout of the temperature. It's so much quicker and safer than a candy thermometer in our experience. The candy thermometer, because it's metal and sits on the side of the pot in the oil, conducts heat and becomes a potential hazard.

HEAT THE OIL AND FRY: Heat the oil over medium heat, checking the temperature every couple of minutes. Make sure your food is ready to go. Once the oil reaches the desired heat, you can add the food to fry. (If you're still not ready to fry yet, turn the heat down to low. Otherwise, you will overheat the oil. When you're ready to fry, turn the heat back to medium, and check the temperature to make sure it's at the level you want.) Add the food without overcrowding. Once you add food, the oil temperature will drop. When the food is done frying, transfer to a tray or plate lined with paper towels. Let the oil come back up to temperature before adding more food.

TIPS: If the oil gets too hot, add a half cup of fresh oil, or more as needed, to even out the temperature. Having tongs and a spider (a wire strainer with a long handle) will help with flipping the food and transferring it to a platter. After you're done frying, let the oil cool completely. If you did a heavy amount of frying, you'll likely have to dispose of the oil. Pour the oil into a container and put it in the trash. If your city has an oil disposal or recycling program, follow the instructions to leave the oil container

out with the recycling. Do *not* pour the oil in the sink. It will build up and cause clogs.

Steaming 101

There are so many great steamed dishes, so it's a good idea to have a steamer. If for no other reason, you want to be able to steam frozen dumplings or bao!

SELECT A POT: Use a pot that's 8 to 11 inches in diameter and that's deep enough to hold 2 to 3 quarts of water. The longer you need to steam, the more water you'll need. If you're steaming for 10 or 15 minutes, about 2 quarts of water should be plenty. For foods that require long steaming time, you will have to check the water level and refill as needed.

LINE THE STEAMER: Get 10-inch perforated parchment liners for the steamer. They come in packs and fit the 10-inch bamboo steamer perfectly. These help prevent your dumplings and buns from sticking. If you're steaming vegetables or proteins, you'll need a heatproof dish that fits in the steamer with at least a half inch of clearance to allow the steam to rise around the rim of the plate.

BOIL WATER AND STEAM: Fill the pot with water. Bring to a boil over high heat. Carefully place the steamer ring in the pot. Place the steamer baskets on top. Steam according to the recipe.

AFTERCARE: After you're done steaming, rinse any residual food or juices off the steamer baskets. Let the steamer pieces air-dry fully on the counter before storing.

幸
福
饗
宴

A WORD ON ETIQUETTE

RESPECT ELDERS: At a celebration where you might have elders as guests, it's important to remember to show respect. Elders should sit in the best position—at the head of a long table or, if the table is round, in the seats where they can see and be seen. You should always serve them first. If you raise a toast, use both hands to raise your glass and bow your head. In formal situations, you would kneel on the floor and prostrate yourself to kowtow (or kētóu in Mandarin). This demonstrates deep respect and reverence.

MIND YOUR CHOPSTICKS: Chopsticks are used for cooking, eating, or serving. They're not drumsticks, conductor batons, hair pins, or other devices that don't involve cooking, eating, or serving. A few other rules to remember:

Don't stab food with chopsticks. If food is unwieldy and you have trouble picking it up with chopsticks, use a spoon to help.

Don't use chopsticks like a fork and knife to break food apart. Just ask for a fork and knife.

Don't use chopsticks to push or pull a plate of food around on the table. If you can't reach something, ask someone to pass it to you.

Don't use your personal chopsticks to dip into food. Use the serving spoon or the serving chopsticks.

Don't cross your chopsticks. It symbolizes death. This is one of our biggest peeves. In so many food photos, people cross their chopsticks, thinking it makes for a more interesting photo. It doesn't. Don't wish death upon people.

Similarly, don't stab your chopsticks into your bowl of food and leave them extended. This also symbolizes death because it resembles the incense you burn for the departed. Do place your chopsticks on chopstick rests or flat on the plate or bowl.

Don't use your chopsticks to gesture or point. If you talk with your hands, put your chopsticks down first.

SERVE YOUR TABLE NEIGHBOR: Serve your table neighbor before serving yourself. This shows hospitality and respect. When you serve yourself, be mindful of the quantity of food you take. When meals are family style, that means everyone should have the opportunity to taste a given dish. If you take a large quantity, the dish may not make it around to everyone before running out.

FIGHT FOR THE BILL: If you're at a restaurant, fighting to pay the bill is a sport. There are memes about this! With mixed groups, it's less of a show. But if you're ever with extended family, it's a race to see who gets the check first.

中國食文化之傳承

PART 1:
CONNECTING WITH CHINESE TRADITIONS

Join us as we celebrate several key holidays and traditions. Specific practices might vary from family to family or region to region. What's universal is that each holiday is a reason to gather, share food, and honor one another—especially our ancestors.

Lunar New Year

First Day, First Month

LUNAR NEW YEAR RECIPES

WHAT'S LUNAR NEW YEAR?

新年快樂!
xīn nián kuài lè!
Happy New Year!

Mom Says

The story of Chinese holidays in our family will always begin with Lunar New Year. Also known as Spring Festival, it holds all the superlatives: the biggest feast, the most family-filled, the loudest, the most festive, and the most delicious. When we reminisce about past dinners, the memories mingle across the years, different homes and dining tables, expanding and contracting as our families have grown or moved. And when the season outside is still dark and cold, this perennial promise of spring gives us an excuse to feast and be together. And to return home to one another.

Lunar New Year is about that homecoming. Where is home? How we've answered that question through the decades and seasons of our lives has changed according to the moment. When my father was still alive, he might have described his familial home in the Henan province of China—a place he barely knew before war sent his family fleeing across the strait to Taiwan. As a young single reporter in Denver, Colorado, I called Columbia, Missouri, home, because that's where my parents and two younger brothers lived. And now, it's our home in a quiet neighborhood in Seattle that has served as the hub for years. It's where my mother tinkers with her garden and blogging, and where Meilee and her brother, Shen, have grown up.

Getting Ready

As the holiday approaches—falling sometime between mid-January and mid-February—we start deep-cleaning the house prior to the date so that we don't risk sweeping away the good luck after the calendar changes. We then hang a few decorations. Enough to acknowledge the moment without overwhelming the house. Though it's sometimes hard to show restraint when all the Asian markets pack their displays to encourage (scare) you into buying all the talismans—just in case. Over the years, it's become easier to buy lucky red decorations through online retailers, so we start getting ads for everything you could possibly think of to stick to your walls or hang from the ceiling. If you visit a major Chinatown, you can find shops that specialize in such emblems of good luck and prosperity.

One of my favorite signals of the season are the mounds of giant pomelo and tangerines with the stems and leaves attached. Tangerines represent gold—and with the leaves, they're just pretty. Pomelos also represent wealth and prosperity. There's something about excavating the sweet-tart pomelo segments from under all that rind that's extra satisfying. By the way, a bowl of tangerines is one of the easiest gifts you can bring as a guest, if you attend a Lunar New Year dinner. Lucky bamboo is another.

Fresh Clothes

Renewal also means new clothes. I usually focus on buying new outfits for our kids. How you decide to interpret this tradition of getting new clothes for New Year's is your choice. For myself, I'd rather spend the money on ingredients for

New York City's Chinatown, Yunhong Chopsticks and Po Wing Hong Food Market.

Pearl River Mart, New York City.

the feast. But, if the urge strikes, I might look for a top that fits the occasion and still allows me the freedom to cook dinner without worrying about ruining it. Shen long ago decided he wasn't comfortable wearing anything with a Mandarin collar, so I let go of that. I'm happy when he wears a polo instead of his usual T-shirt.

Meilee, luckily, will wear a qipao at least for Lunar New Year. On a recent visit to New York City's Chinatown, we went to Pearl River Mart, where Meilee fell in love with a cropped qipao top and a pair of men's pants. I appreciate the contemporary take on some traditional pieces. This outfit could not have been more perfect for Meilee's current sensibilities, and it undoubtedly will show up at the next Lunar New Year. She's also tall enough now that she can wear my mother's custom qipao from the 1960s. I've never had the figure for a qipao, so it delights me that Meilee can connect with her lau lau through these dresses.

MEILEE: It was really cool to think about all the history the dress I was wearing held. Although it was scratchy and uncomfortable (because it was unlined and I didn't have a slip), it still felt good to be the next person to inherit this piece of family history.

RED ENVELOPES AND LUCKY MONEY

Red envelopes come in countless designs that may include different symbols of good luck, longevity, prosperity, and good fortune. Some

MEILEE SAYS: When I was younger, I never fully knew what these lucky dollars represented. I was always tormented by the idea of having an untouchable dollar bill I couldn't spend on some trinket or toy. As I got older, I learned about the symbolism and that these dollars are meant to represent good fortune. I did not receive the money as if it were an allowance, but rather a blessing of good luck. So my perspective has shifted a lot, and I feel grateful my lau lau has passed these on to us.

designs incorporate the current zodiac year. The long envelopes fit unfolded bills. The smaller envelopes require you to fold up the money. We use red envelopes throughout the year for other celebrations and milestones, such as graduations, birthdays, weddings, births. Sometimes the messages on the envelopes match the occasion. Be sure to ask someone who can read Chinese characters to confirm you're buying the appropriate red envelopes. Generally, around Lunar New Year, shops stock the right ones for the holiday.

The US Treasury issues dollar bills at Lunar New Year with serial numbers that start with 8888. Eight is a lucky number because the word for eight, *ba*, sounds like the *fa* in *fa cai*, which means "get rich." For years, my mother has ordered these lucky dollar bills for all the grandkids. We have stacks of these!

THE FEAST

My sweet spot is cooking, of course. The feast planning is directly proportional to my level of ambition and what the circumstances demand: One or two celebrations? Small or large group? Family only or with friends? There have been years when I end up making two meals because the holiday falls on an inconvenient school/work night. (If we were overseas, everyone would have the Lunar New Year holiday time off.) So I make a mini celebration for the five of us on the day of and a subsequent grand dinner on an agreeable weekend night, with eight to ten—or more—dishes. One year, the kids requested dim sum for dinner. I obliged, but it was so much work to make several different dumplings, scallion pancakes, sticky rice in lotus leaf, and pork buns that I was too tired to eat. I haven't done that menu since. Ideally, the New Year's menu has a balance of types of dishes, flavors, textures, cooking methods—and symbolic meaning. Striking that balance can make a difference in the vibe of the day. For example, I think about these characteristics:

Braised and simmered dishes can be made ahead and easily reheated. Some stir-fries also can hold at room temperature. You can make dumplings a day ahead, freeze them, and then cook them frozen. I pick dishes that allow me to stagger the prep times so that not everything requires last-minute cooking.

What appears on our menu is a combination of family favorites and the must-serve lucky foods. What makes a given food lucky might be related to its shape or color or that its name is a homophone for a fortuitous saying. For example, a whole fish represents continued prosperity because there's a saying that roughly translates to "wishing you have fish every year." The golden color of tangerines harkens back to the gold ingot of the day and thus means wealth. Rice cake, or nian gao, literally means "sticky cake." But *nian gao* is also a homophone for "stacking up the years"—or wishing you longevity. Watermelon seeds, which you can buy in packs like sunflower seeds, and lotus represent fertility and family.

It's important to make more than enough food not only to demonstrate abundance and richness, but also because we eat leftovers the next day.

Day Before	Morning Of	Afternoon	1 to 1 ½ Hours Before	30 Minutes Before
Make dumplings and scallion pancakes to freeze	Buy duck from the barbecue shop, prep vegetables and proteins, prep braises	Start braising, group ingredients by dish	Start heating up braised dishes, boil noodles, plate duck and other items that can hold at room temp	Cook dumplings and pancakes; while people munch on those, cook the stir-fries

幸
福
饗
宴

Method	Texture	Flavor	Type	Meaning
• stir-fried	• tender	• salty	• vegetable	• good fortune
• deep-fried	• crispy	• sweet	• protein	• good luck
• steamed	• bouncy (chewy)	• spicy	• seafood	• prosperity
• braised	• soft	• acidic	• noodle	• longevity
• simmered	• juicy	• umami	• dumpling	• family
• seared	• flaky		• bun	• togetherness
	• spongy		• rice	• wealth
	• sticky			• abundance

You're not supposed to use knives or anything that might cut your good luck, which means no cooking! This isn't the only superstition. You're supposed to set off firecrackers at midnight to scare away bad luck and celebrate the coming year. We can't set off firecrackers where we live, so we have to use noisemakers. It's not always easy to follow every holiday practice.

It would be hard to claim that we have a molecular understanding of the most traditional of traditions. When you grow up where Lunar New Year isn't a part of the language and culture, new roots have to sprout and find a way to cling and thrive. In a midwestern small town or even in Seattle, the collective energy, expectations, and reverence for the holiday doesn't reach the same pitch as in Asia or in larger Chinatowns like in New York or San Francisco. We do the best we can and celebrate however we decide to celebrate.

CHINESE ZODIAC YEARS

We won't get into the full description of the Chinese zodiac and astrology because that information fills volumes. You can read about it online or in numerous books—and even on cheesy placemats you sometimes find at neighborhood Chinese restaurants. The animals always appear in the order listed here. This chart is a reference for when Lunar New Year takes place through 2044. The first date represents New Year's Day. To ring in the Year of the Snake in 2025, for example, you'd hold the New Year's Eve feast on January 28, 2025.

Year	Lunar New Year's Eve
2025/Snake	January 28, 2025
2026/Horse	February 16, 2026
2027/Sheep	February 5, 2027
2028/Monkey	January 25, 2028
2029/Rooster	February 12, 2029
2030/Dog	February 2, 2030
2031/Pig	January 22, 2031

RAT

January 25, 2020–February 11, 2021
February 11, 2032–January 30, 2033

OX

February 12, 2021–January 31, 2022
January 31, 2033–February 18, 2034

TIGER

February 1, 2022–January 21, 2023
February 19, 2034–February 7, 2035

RABBIT

January 22, 2023–February 9, 2024
February 8, 2035–January 27, 2036

DRAGON

February 10, 2024–January 28, 2025
January 28, 2036–February 14, 2037

SNAKE

January 29, 2025–February 16, 2026
February 15, 2037–February 3, 2038

HORSE

February 17, 2026–February 5, 2027
February 4, 2038–January 23, 2039

SHEEP

February 6, 2027–January 25, 2028
January 24, 2039–February 11, 2040

MONKEY

January 26, 2028–February 12, 2029
February 12, 2040–January 31, 2041

ROOSTER

February 13, 2029–February 2, 2030
February 1, 2041–January 21, 2042

DOG

February 3, 2030–January 22, 2031
January 22, 2042–February 9, 2043

PIG

January 23, 2031–February 10, 2032
February 10, 2043–January 29, 2044

幸
福
饗
宴

MEILEE'S PERSPECTIVE: BEYOND RED ENVELOPES

When I was younger, Lunar New Year was about red-envelope money and seeing my cousins, especially Lucie, who was born in the same Year of the Dog as I was. I anxiously waited at the window, watching cars pass and hoping my cousins would be in one of them. When they finally arrived, I, too excited to put on shoes, would run out to the car to hug them. We didn't see each other very often, so I needed to make the most of our family dinners.

We would weave through the maze of adults in the kitchen and stomp around in Lau Lau's (Grandma's) room, which had become a playroom for all of us. We would play with the toy kitchen, Hot Wheels cars, or even just our imaginations. Sometimes, we went on our iPads and made movies together. The smell of the food being made would creep into the room, making all of us wonder when it would finally be time to eat. No matter where we went or what we did, joy and laughter followed, smiles wide across our faces.

At dinner, we would get to have sparkling cider, which we would all pretend was champagne to be more adultlike. We were all picky eaters, so our plates were all the same: rice, dumplings, and scallion pancakes. Afterward was the moment we had been waiting for all night. Our families would give us our red envelopes. Receiving them always made me feel older because I had to be responsible for the money and keep track of it. My cousins and I would

gather to compare how much money we got—the older kids always getting a few dollars more. Later that night, I would lie in bed and imagine all the toys and treasures I could now afford.

Today, I am seventeen. The pandemic changed how I think about what the holiday means to me. It took away my sense of community and connection despite trying to keep it alive over Zoom. I've learned this: While the money is nice to pay for gas or new makeup, Lunar New Year means so much more. It is a holiday about putting our busy lives aside and appreciating being together. At the table is a delicious feast with a dish specially made for each of us—spring rolls for Lucie, chicken for me, and red-braised pork belly for my uncles. The room is always loud with conversation and laughter. There is so much to be grateful for, and it is important to celebrate that. You can feel the warmth of love fill the area all night.

As we grow up, Lunar New Year will forever hold a special place in our hearts. Watching my two youngest cousins, Duncan and Fletcher, in their grade school days fills me with an overwhelming sense of affection as they jump through the house, leaving trails of laughter behind them. I'm confident that, just like the rest of us, they'll realize that Lunar New Year is about more than just the symbolic red envelopes. It's about the warmth of family and community, the embrace of tradition, and the connection that weaves us together.

陰
曆
新
年

Crispy spring rolls are a popular appetizer across many cuisines. They're straightforward to make and the filling can contain almost any combination of ingredients. In many restaurants, the filling tends to feature shredded green cabbage and can get mushy. We prefer to have discernible ingredients that still have texture. Basically, if we can stir-fry the mixture, it can go in a spring roll wrapper.

■ Preheat a wok over high heat until wisps of smoke rise from the surface. Swirl the oil into the wok. Add the cabbage, bean sprouts, carrots, mushrooms, and onions and stir-fry the vegetables for 1 to 2 minutes, or until the cabbage softens. Add the soy sauce and stir-fry for 1 to 2 minutes more, or until all the vegetables are just cooked through. Drizzle with sesame oil and stir to combine. Transfer the filling to a large bowl and set aside to cool while you set up to wrap the spring rolls.

■ Position a sheet of spring roll wrapper with a corner toward you so that the sheet is shaped like a diamond. Place about ¼ cup filling about 2 inches above the bottom corner of the wrapper. Fold the bottom corner up over the filling. To create the tube shape, curl your fingers on top of the wrapper and filling and gently pull toward you to tighten the wrapper around the filling. Roll up about halfway up the diamond. Fold the right-side "flap" over the filling, then the left side. It will now look like an envelope. Brush the top flap with egg and finish rolling to seal. Repeat with the remaining wrappers and filling. ⟶

炸春捲

CRISPY SPRING ROLLS

VEGETARIAN

EFFORT ●●●

MAKES ABOUT 1 DOZEN

2 tablespoons vegetable oil, plus more for frying

3 cups thinly sliced Chinese cabbage (or regular green cabbage)

1 cup bean sprouts

½ cup grated carrot

½ cup thinly sliced fresh or dried shiitake mushrooms (soak dried mushrooms in warm water for at least 1 hour to reconstitute)

2 green onions, finely chopped

3 tablespoons soy sauce

½ teaspoon sesame oil

1 package 8-inch spring roll wrappers, such as Wei-Chuan or TYJ brands

1 large egg, beaten

Sweet-and-Sour Sauce (page 188) or store-bought sweet chili sauce, for serving

■ Place a few layers of paper towel on a small platter or a large dinner plate and set aside. In a deep pan, add about 1½ inches of vegetable oil and heat over medium-high heat to 375 degrees F on an instant-read thermometer. In batches, fry the rolls for 1 to 2 minutes per side, or until the skin is evenly golden. If the skin browns too quickly, then the oil is too hot. Adjust the temperature as needed. Since the filling is already cooked through, the goal is to crisp the skin.

■ Drain on the paper-towel-lined plate. Serve with store-bought sweet chili sauce, Sweet-and-Sour Sauce, or your choice of condiments.

MOM SAYS: To tame the fear factor of frying, keep these tips in mind:

- Use a deep-sided pot, such as a Dutch oven or a saucepot. This will help contain some of the splattering. The diameter of the pot can vary, but a 6- to 8-inch pot is a good starting point.

- Fry in batches. If you put too much food into the oil, the oil might bubble over, and it also brings down the temperature of the oil. If the temperature of the oil gets too low, the food will start to soak up too much oil.

- A digital thermometer is key to monitoring the oil temperature. After each batch, check the oil temperature and make sure it has time to heat back up to 375 degrees F before starting another batch.

陰
曆
新
年

At Lunar New Year, you make dumplings to eat just before midnight to say goodbye to the year and usher in the new. The bulbous shape of the dumpling resembles the shape of the ancient Chinese currency called a tael. Our family serves dumplings with our main feast—since we prefer not to eat such a filling food so late at night.

- To make the dough, place the flour in a large mixing bowl. Add the water and, using a rubber spatula or wooden spoon, stir the water and flour together. Continue to stir gently until a ball of dough starts to form. Start kneading the dough to make a ball. The dough should feel slightly tacky but not damp. Cover the dough with a damp towel or plastic wrap and let it rest for a minimum of 20 minutes.

- To make the filling, combine the ground pork, Chinese cabbage, green onions, soy sauce, minced ginger, sesame oil, and white pepper in a medium bowl and mix well. Set aside.

- To make the wrappers, divide the dough in half. Roll each half into a rope that's about ¾ inch in diameter and about 18 inches or so in length. Cut each rope into pieces that are about ¾ inch thick (or about 9 or 10 grams). Dust your work surface and the dough pieces with flour. Roll each piece into a ball, then press it between your palms into a silver-dollar-size disk. With a 10- or 12-inch Chinese dowel-style rolling pin (available in Asian markets or online), roll each disk into a flat circle about 3 inches in diameter. Dust with flour as needed to prevent sticking. Don't worry about making a perfect circle.

- Place a dollop of filling, about a teaspoon or so, into the center of a wrapper. Fold the round wrapper in half over the center into a half-moon shape and pinch shut along the edges. The dough should be just sticky enough to seal without using water or egg. Repeat until you have used up all the dough or you run out of filling. ⟶

豬肉白菜水餃

PORK AND CHINESE CABBAGE DUMPLINGS

EFFORT ● ● ●
MAKES ABOUT 48 DUMPLINGS

FOR THE DOUGH:

2½ cups unbleached all-purpose flour, plus more for dusting

¾ cup warm tap water

FOR THE FILLING:

1 pound ground pork, preferably Kurobuta pork (or another type that's not too lean)

2½ cups loosely packed finely chopped Chinese cabbage

1 green onion, finely chopped

2 tablespoons soy sauce

1 teaspoon minced fresh ginger

1 teaspoon sesame oil

¼ teaspoon white pepper powder

Dumpling Dipping Sauce (recipe follows)

■ To cook, fill a large soup pot with 4 quarts of water and bring to a boil over high heat. Set a 1-cup measuring cup filled with cold water next to the stove, within easy reach. When the water starts to boil, carefully add about half the prepared dumplings, or only as many as your pot can accommodate without overcrowding. Return to a boil and cook for about 5 minutes. You may have to fish out a dumpling and cut it open to confirm. Keep a close watch on the water as it will likely bubble over. Add a quick splash of the cold water to help calm down the boil and adjust the heat as needed. You want a steady boil that doesn't boil over the top of the pot. The dumplings are done when they puff up, float, and the skins are slightly translucent. Use a large slotted spoon or a spider strainer to transfer the cooked dumplings to a platter. Serve with Dumpling Dipping Sauce.

MOM SAYS: If you need a tutorial on how to pleat dumplings, search on YouTube for my name and "dumplings" to get helpful videos. For the ground pork, you can buy unseasoned bulk sausage to get a mixture that has more marbling.

Dumpling Dipping Sauce

EFFORT ●○○

MAKES ABOUT ½ CUP

⅓ cup soy sauce

2 tablespoons rice vinegar

1 tablespoon chopped cilantro

1 green onion, finely chopped

2 cloves garlic, finely chopped

1 teaspoon minced fresh ginger

1 teaspoon chili sauce or chili crisp (optional)

■ Mix all the ingredients in a small bowl. If you have time, let it sit for at least 30 minutes to allow the flavors to meld together. The longer the mixture rests, the more intense the flavor becomes. Once mixed, the sauce will keep in a sealed container in the refrigerator for up to a week.

幸
福
饗
宴

素鍋貼
VEGETABLE POTSTICKERS

VEGAN

EFFORT ● ● ●

MAKES ABOUT 40 DUMPLINGS

2 teaspoons vegetable oil, plus more for frying

2 green onions, chopped

1 small zucchini, grated

4 cups finely chopped Chinese cabbage

2 cups finely chopped baby bok choy

¾ cup grated carrot

6 medium dried shiitake mushrooms, soaked in warm water for 2 to 3 hours, stemmed and finely diced, or fresh cremini mushrooms

1 tablespoon soy sauce

½ teaspoon kosher salt

1 teaspoon sesame oil

1 package store-bought potsticker or gyoza wrappers

Dumpling Dipping Sauce (page 58)

While boiled dumplings are the most traditional for Lunar New Year, our family loves potstickers (pan-fried dumplings). This recipe uses store-bought wrappers, but if you want to make yours from scratch, follow the dough instructions in the recipe for Pork and Chinese Cabbage Dumplings (page 57). A quick note about store-bought wrappers: the number of wrappers in a package can vary, so the yield on this recipe is approximate. Also, you can use other types of leafy Asian greens as well as hardier greens such as kale or chard.

■ Preheat a wok over high heat until wisps of smoke rise from the surface. Swirl the oil into the wok. Add the green onions and zucchini and stir-fry for about 30 seconds. Add the cabbage, baby bok choy, carrots, and mushrooms. Stir-fry, making sure to combine the ingredients well, for about 3 minutes. Add the soy sauce and salt and stir-fry for 1 minute. Drizzle on the sesame oil. Stir to combine. Turn off the heat and transfer the vegetable mixture to a plate and set aside to cool for 15 to 20 minutes.

■ Set up your dumpling-making station with the filling, stack of wrappers, and a small dish with about ¼ cup water. Line a baking sheet with parchment paper and set aside.

■ To make the dumplings, dip your index finger in the water and brush the outer edge of the wrapper. Repeat until the outer edge is moistened. Place 1 heaping teaspoon of the filling in the center of the wrapper. Fold the wrapper over the filling into a half-moon shape. Match the edges together and press as if you were sealing an envelope. Holding the sealed edge of the dumpling between your fingers, set it on its spine and gently wiggle it as you push down so that the dumpling will stand up. Place the completed dumpling on the parchment-lined baking sheet. Repeat to prepare the remaining dumplings.

■ Preheat an 8- or 9-inch nonstick skillet over medium heat for about 1 minute. (If you have a bigger or smaller skillet, that's fine. Adjust the oil amount as needed.) Avoid high heat, which can cause the nonstick coating to deteriorate. Add enough vegetable oil to generously coat the entire surface of the pan and create a slight pool of oil (about ⅛ inch deep). This may seem like a lot of oil, but it will help you create that telltale crispy potsticker crust.

■ Carefully arrange the dumplings in a single layer in the skillet, flat side down. Add ½ cup water to the skillet and cover immediately. Cook for 7 to 9 minutes, or until the water has evaporated and the bottoms of the dumplings have turned a golden brown. The cooking time may vary slightly depending on your stove. Adjust the heat as needed. Place cooked dumplings on a serving platter. Serve with Dumpling Dipping Sauce.

MOM SAYS: There are a lot of brands of store-bought dumpling wrappers. If you can get to an Asian market that has a great selection of Chinese ingredients, look for packages that specify they're for potstickers. New Hong Kong brand, for example, offers dumpling wrappers in different thicknesses for different cooking methods. You might also find labels that say "gyoza"—which is the Japanese term for dumplings. Those will work fine too, though they may be thin and less forgiving to work with.

陰
曆
新
年

Holiday or not, scallion pancakes are a family favorite, so we always make them for any gathering. Scallions, green onions, or spring onions are different names for the same ingredient. In the context of Lunar New Year, spring onions symbolize the coming of the spring season. Some families hang a stalk of spring onion over their door for good luck.

蔥油餅 (純素)
SCALLION PANCAKES

VEGAN
EFFORT ●●○
MAKES 4 (6-INCH) PANCAKES

2½ cups unbleached all-purpose flour, plus more for dusting

¾ cup warm water (about 95 to 100 degrees F)

7 tablespoons vegetable oil, divided

2 teaspoons kosher salt, divided

4 green onions, finely chopped

Dumpling Dipping Sauce (page 58)

- To make the dough, place the flour in a mixing bowl. Add the water and, using a rubber spatula or wooden spoon, stir the water and flour together. Continue to stir gently until a ball of dough starts to form. Start kneading the dough to make a ball. The dough should feel slightly tacky but not damp. Cover the dough with a damp towel or plastic wrap and let it rest for a minimum of 20 minutes and up to several hours.

- Set up the assembly line. Place 2 tablespoons of the vegetable oil in a small bowl and set a small pastry brush next to it. In another small dish, place the 2 teaspoons of kosher salt. Set the chopped green onions in a small bowl next to the salt.

- Divide the dough into quarters. Lightly dust your work surface. Roll one piece of dough out to about 8½ inches in diameter. Brush a coating of oil onto the dough. Sprinkle about ½ teaspoon salt across the oiled dough, making sure to sprinkle from a height of 8 to 10 inches above the dough. This helps to distribute the salt more evenly across the surface.

- Spread 2 to 3 tablespoons of green onions across the dough. Starting from the bottom edge of the round of dough, roll the dough tightly into a tube. Then take one end of the tube and coil it into a tightly wound coil. Gently stretch and tuck the end under the coil. Roll the coiled dough flat until it's about 6½ inches in diameter and about ⅛ inch thick. Repeat with the remaining sections of dough.

- Preheat an 8-inch skillet over medium-low heat for about 1 minute. Add 2 tablespoons of oil and heat for about 5 seconds, or until it starts to shimmer. Add a pancake and fry for 1½ to 2 minutes on each side, or until golden. Remove the pancake and set aside on a plate lined with paper towels. Add 1 tablespoon of oil to the pan before cooking each of the remaining pancakes. Cut the pancakes into wedges and serve with the dipping sauce.

幸
福
饗
宴

素十錦
LUCKY MIXED VEGETABLES

VEGAN

EFFORT ●○○

MAKES 4 SERVINGS, FAMILY STYLE

1 tablespoon vegetable oil

1 cup bean sprouts

1 cup sliced (¼ inch thick) celery

1 cup sliced (¼ inch thick) mushrooms, such as shiitake (soak dried shiitake in warm water for at least 1 hour to reconstitute)

1 cup enoki mushrooms, trimmed and separated

1 cup sliced (¼ inch thick) carrot

1 cup sliced (¼ inch thick) Chinese cabbage

1 cup sliced (¼ inch thick) baby bok choy

8 snow peas, trimmed and cut into ½-inch segments

1 tablespoon soy sauce, plus more as needed

1 tablespoon water

¼ teaspoon sesame oil

⅛ teaspoon white pepper powder

When you're making a big feast, you want to have some dishes that are quick to make to balance the ones that take more effort. This dish fits the bill. Eight is a lucky number in Chinese culture because the character for *eight* is a homophone for *prosperity*. This stir-fry includes eight kinds of vegetables. As long as you consider how well the textures and flavors play together, you can use almost any combination of vegetables you prefer.

■ Preheat a wok over high heat until wisps of smoke rise from the surface. Swirl in the vegetable oil and heat for a few seconds until it starts to shimmer. Add all the vegetables: bean sprouts, celery, shiitake, enoki, carrots, Chinese cabbage, baby bok choy, and snow peas. Stir-fry for about 2 minutes and then add the soy sauce and water. Stir to combine. Add the sesame oil, white pepper, and stir-fry for 1 to 2 minutes to combine. Turn off the heat. Taste for seasoning. If it isn't salty enough, stir in another teaspoon or so of soy sauce. Transfer to a serving dish.

MOM SAYS: In a pinch, you could use a bagged salad—such as a slaw mix—to minimize some of the prep work.

陰
曆
新
年

Rice cake is symbolic because the Mandarin characters for *nian gao* are homophones for the words that mean "sticky" and "year." So eating rice cake comes with the wish for longevity. Rice cakes are available sliced, marble-shaped, and in batons. You can work with whatever shape you'd like, but we're using sliced for this recipe. Look for these in the refrigerated noodle section at Asian markets.

雞肉青菜炒年糕
STIR-FRIED RICE CAKE
with Chicken and Vegetables

EFFORT ● ○ ○

MAKES 4 SERVINGS, FAMILY STYLE

2 cups sliced rice cake

3 cups hot tap water

6 ounces boneless, skinless chicken breast

1 tablespoon plus 1 teaspoon soy sauce, divided

1 tablespoon cornstarch

2 tablespoons vegetable oil, divided

2 cups sliced baby bok choy

½ cup sliced (¼ inch thick) fresh or dried shiitake mushrooms (soak dried shiitake in warm water for at least 1 hour to reconstitute)

½ cup bean sprouts (optional)

¼ cup sliced (¼ inch thick) carrots

1 tablespoon hoisin sauce

½ teaspoon sesame oil

■ In a medium bowl, soak the rice cake in the hot water for 2 to 3 minutes, then drain all but about ½ cup of the water. Set aside.

■ Cut the chicken breast lengthwise into two to three strips, about 1½ inches wide, or about the size of chicken tenders. Then slice each strip of chicken crosswise into slivers. The exact size of the slivers is not as important as keeping the pieces relatively uniform. In a small bowl, combine the chicken and 1 teaspoon of the soy sauce, and mix well. Add the cornstarch and mix well again. Preheat a wok over high heat until wisps of smoke rise from the surface. Add 1 tablespoon of the vegetable oil and heat for 5 seconds. Spread the chicken in a thin layer in the wok. Sear the slivers of chicken for about 30 seconds, then stir-fry the chicken for about 1 minute until cooked through. Turn off the heat. Transfer the chicken to a small bowl and set aside. Rinse the wok and dry with a towel.

■ Return the wok to the stove over high heat. Add the remaining 1 tablespoon vegetable oil and heat for 5 seconds. Add the baby bok choy, mushrooms, bean sprouts, and carrots and stir-fry for 1 minute to combine. Add the rice cake and reserved water. Stir to combine. Add the remaining 1 tablespoon soy sauce and hoisin sauce. Stir-fry for 2 minutes, or until the rice cake has fully reconstituted and is soft. Finish with the sesame oil. Turn off the heat and transfer to a serving dish.

MOM SAYS: You can easily turn this recipe into a hearty soup by adding some broth to it. It'd be great as a meal for two. You can change the protein too, or make it vegetarian. Your choice!

素炒蘿曼萵苣

STIR-FRIED ROMAINE

VEGAN

EFFORT ●○○

MAKES 4 SERVINGS, FAMILY STYLE

1 head romaine lettuce (about 1 pound)

1 tablespoon vegetable oil

2 to 3 cloves garlic, finely minced or crushed

1 tablespoon soy sauce

1 to 2 tablespoons water, as needed

½ teaspoon sesame oil

⅛ teaspoon white pepper powder (optional)

Lettuce symbolizes prosperity because the characters in Mandarin are homophones for the phrase "growing your fortune." Romaine is great because it's hardy enough to withstand stir-frying but still delicate to eat. Like any other stir-fried greens, romaine is most delicious when treated simply. If you want to spice this up, feel free to add chili sauce or fresh peppers to taste.

■ Cut the romaine in quarters lengthwise through the core. Cut out the core. Slice the quarters crosswise into pieces that are about 1½ inches wide. This doesn't have to be exact. What's important is that the pieces are relatively the same size.

■ Preheat a wok over high heat until wisps of smoke rise from the surface. Add the vegetable oil and garlic and stir for about 5 seconds. Be quick so you don't burn the garlic. Add the lettuce and stir-fry for about 2 minutes, or until the leafy parts start to wilt and no longer look raw. Swirl in the soy sauce and stir. If the lettuce looks too dry, add 1 to 2 tablespoons water. Add the sesame oil and white pepper. Give it one last stir to combine. Turn off the heat and transfer to a serving dish.

MOM SAYS: All vegetables have moisture. Lettuces and other leafy greens tend to hold moisture that releases when you apply heat. But if the greens aren't in their freshest state (maybe they sat in the fridge for a couple of extra days and have started to wilt), you may have to add a tiny bit of water to help the stir-fry.

幸
福
饗
宴

糯米雞 + 香腸
RICE-COOKER STICKY RICE
with Chicken and Chinese Sausage

EFFORT ●○○

MAKES 4 TO 6 SERVINGS, FAMILY STYLE

3 tablespoons soy sauce, divided

2 tablespoons hoisin sauce

1 tablespoon oyster sauce

6 ounces boneless, skinless chicken thighs, cut into 1-inch pieces

2 teaspoons cornstarch

2 teaspoons vegetable oil

1 green onion, finely chopped

3 medium dried shiitake mushrooms, soaked in warm water for 2 to 3 hours, cut into ½-inch dice

1 Chinese sausage, sliced ¼ inch thick on the bias

1½ cups sweet rice, such as Sho-Chiku-Bai

1½ cups water

Sticky rice, similar to rice cake, symbolizes longevity. Our family loves sticky rice in lotus leaf, but it's a bit of a process to make it. This is our shortcut version. While it doesn't have the aroma of the lotus leaf, it definitely is less labor-intensive to make.

■ In a small bowl, combine 2 tablespoons of the soy sauce, the hoisin sauce, and the oyster sauce. Stir well, then set aside.

■ Place the chicken in another bowl. Add the remaining 1 tablespoon soy sauce. Mix well. Add the cornstarch and mix well again. In a medium skillet, heat the vegetable oil over medium-high heat. Add the chicken, using a spatula to break up the pieces. Let sear for about 30 seconds or so, flip the pieces and sear for another 30 seconds. Add the green onions, mushrooms, sausage, and the sauce mixture. Stir to combine. Turn off the heat and move the skillet off the hot burner.

■ To wash the rice: Place the rice in a bowl. Cover with cool water. Use your hand or a rice spatula to agitate the rice. Drain and repeat two more times. Transfer the rice to the pot of a rice cooker. Add 1½ cups water, making sure the rice is evenly distributed in the pot.

■ Add the chicken mixture to the center of the rice, but don't stir. Close the lid to the rice cooker and set it to cook sweet rice. When cooked and ready to serve, make sure to include bits of the chicken and sausage with the rice. Feel free to top with additional condiments, such as soy sauce, chili sauce, or chili crisp, as desired.

> **MOM SAYS:** You can switch the proteins, add vegetables, and adjust the seasonings to your liking. The filling—in this case, it's a topping—is flexible.

陰
曆
新
年

Gai lan, or Chinese broccoli, symbolizes harmony. While you could serve gai lan on its own or combine it with any number of proteins, we're featuring shrimp. Shrimp can be expensive sometimes, so it makes sense that you might want to save it for a special occasion like Lunar New Year. A note about sizing: The numbers, such as 26/30, signify how many shrimp there are per pound. So 26/30 means that there are 26 to 30 shrimp per pound. The larger the number, the smaller the shrimp.

蒜香芥藍蝦

GARLIC SHRIMP
with Gai Lan

EFFORT ● ○ ○

MAKES 4 SERVINGS, FAMILY STYLE

8 to 12 ounces peeled and deveined shrimp (preferably 26/30 size; see headnote)

1½ tablespoons soy sauce, divided

1 tablespoon cornstarch

About 4 ounces gai lan

6 to 8 plump cloves garlic, crushed

2 tablespoons water

1 tablespoon hoisin sauce

1 teaspoon Thai-style sweet chili sauce (optional)

1 tablespoon plus 2 teaspoons vegetable oil, divided

■ In a medium bowl, combine the shrimp with 1 tablespoon of the soy sauce. Mix well to coat. Then add the cornstarch and mix well to coat. Set aside.

■ Trim about ½ inch off the ends of the gai lan stalks to remove any dried bits. Also remove any leaves that look ragged or are starting to yellow. Starting on the stalk end, slice into ¼-inch pieces. When you get to the leafy ends, you can cut them into roughly 1-inch pieces. You should have about 2 cups. Place gai lan in a medium bowl and set aside.

■ In a small bowl, combine the garlic, water, hoisin sauce, sweet chili sauce, and the remaining ½ tablespoon soy sauce. Stir well to combine, making sure the hoisin sauce isn't stuck to the bottom of the bowl. Set aside.

■ To parcook the shrimp: Preheat a wok over medium heat until wisps of smoke rise from the surface. Swirl in 1 tablespoon of the vegetable oil and heat for a few seconds until it starts to shimmer. Add the shrimp and spread out into a single layer. Sear for about 30 seconds or so. Flip and sear for another 30 seconds or so. Then stir-fry for about 1 minute. Turn off the heat. Scoop out the shrimp back into the bowl and set aside. The shrimp will not be cooked through yet.

■ Scrape off any bits and pieces on the surface of the wok. If needed, give it a light scrub and rinse in the sink, being mindful that the wok is still very hot. ⟶

■ Return the wok to high heat. Swirl in the remaining 2 teaspoons vegetable oil. Let heat for 5 to 10 seconds. Add the gai lan and stir-fry for about 1 minute, or until the greens start to glisten. Add the shrimp and stir-fry to combine. Swirl in the sauce mixture and stir-fry for 1 to 2 minutes, or until the sauce evenly coats all the ingredients. Don't linger too long or you risk overcooking the shrimp. Turn off the heat and transfer to a serving dish.

MOM SAYS: There are so many varieties of shrimp you can buy. This recipe works with any of them, so don't fret if you don't find the exact size. You can use fresh or previously frozen shrimp, peeled or shell-on. If it's shell-on, you will have to peel the shrimp and devein them (see page 35) before you add them to the stir-fry.

陰
曆
新
年

For Lunar New Year, it's customary to serve whole chicken to represent unity. We typically serve chicken in a stir-fry to be in the spirit of the tradition if not the letter of the tradition. Meilee could live on chicken and rice, so this dish is a go-to. It's straight-up chicken and sauce. But don't worry: like we do, you can pair this stir-fry with any number of vegetable dishes—including the options in the Stir-Fries Make Great Holiday Side Dishes chapter (page 196).

攻力式炒雞絲

MEILEE'S STIR-FRIED CHICKEN

EFFORT ●○○

MAKES 4 SERVINGS, FAMILY STYLE

1 pound boneless, skinless chicken breast

2 tablespoons soy sauce, divided

1 tablespoon cornstarch

2 tablespoons water

1 to 2 tablespoons hoisin sauce

1 teaspoon finely minced or crushed fresh garlic

1 teaspoon sugar

1 tablespoon vegetable oil

■ Cut the chicken breast lengthwise into two to three strips, about 1½ inches wide, or about the size of chicken tenders. Then slice each strip of chicken crosswise into slivers. The exact size of the slivers is not as important as keeping the pieces relatively uniform. Place the chicken in a medium bowl and mix in 1 tablespoon of the soy sauce. Add the cornstarch and mix well. Set aside. In a small bowl, combine the remaining 1 tablespoon soy sauce, water, hoisin sauce to taste, garlic, and sugar. Set aside.

■ Preheat a wok over high heat until wisps of smoke rise from the surface. Swirl the oil into the wok. Immediately add the chicken to the wok and, using your wok spatula, spread the chicken out into a single layer. Let the chicken sear for about 30 seconds. Then stir the chicken and spread out again, letting it sear for about 15 seconds. Now, actively stir-fry for about 1 minute. Swirl in the sauce mixture and stir-fry for another minute, or until the sauce is well combined with the chicken and looks glossy. Turn off the heat and transfer to a serving dish.

MOM SAYS: You can buy a pack of "stir-fry chicken" from the grocery store. Sometimes, the chicken pieces are pretty thick, so cut them smaller before using. You can also use boneless, skinless chicken thighs instead of breasts.

A whole fish at Lunar New Year represents prosperity and continued good fortune in the years to come. For this recipe, you'll need a steamer large enough to accommodate a whole fish. You don't want to cut the fish in half, because that would be bad luck! Also, when you serve the fish, point the head toward the most distinguished guest at the table. In our home, that would be Lau Lau—or Grandma. Finally, when you're done serving one side of the fish, do not flip it. Instead, lift the bone to separate it from the other fillet. Flipping the fish represents sinking a boat, and we don't want to mess with good fortune.

■ Set up your steamer (see page 37) over medium heat. In a medium bowl, mix the green onions and ginger. Put half the mixture in another bowl. Set aside.

■ Score the fish by gently making three or four cuts along the body from the dorsal fin to the belly. Your knife should graze the bone but not cut through it. Repeat on the other side. If you have two fish, repeat these steps for the second fish.

■ Line a steam-proof dish with a piece of parchment paper, cutting the parchment to size as needed. After steaming, the parchment will help you transfer the fish to your serving platter. (If you have a larger steamer, you could use a glass pie plate, for example.) Place the fish on the parchment-lined dish. Carefully sprinkle some salt into the slits. Using half the ginger-onion mixture, place a few strands of ginger and onion in all the slits on both sides. Carefully lift the lid of the steamer, making sure to position yourself away from the burst of steam that will rise. Place the fish in the steamer, cover, and let steam for about 15 minutes.

■ Meanwhile, combine the remaining ginger and onions with the soy sauce, wine, and vegetable oil in a small pot. Heat over medium-high heat. Once it comes to a boil, reduce the heat to low. Keep the sauce over low heat while the fish steams. ⟶

蔥薑蒸全魚
STEAMED GINGER-SCALLION BRANZINO

EFFORT ●●○

MAKES 4 TO 6 SERVINGS, FAMILY STYLE

6 green onions, cut into 3-inch julienne (see page 33)

½ cup very finely julienned fresh ginger, divided

1 whole branzino, about 1½ pounds (ask the fish butcher to clean and scale the fish)

1 to 2 teaspoons kosher salt

3 tablespoons soy sauce

2 tablespoons Shaoxing wine or a dry white wine (optional)

2 tablespoons vegetable oil

Roughly chopped fresh cilantro leaves (about ½ cup)

■ Once the 15 minutes are up, check the fish for doneness: Turn off the heat and carefully lift the lid of the steamer and set aside. Using the tip of a sharp knife, gently probe the flesh at the thickest part of the fish. If it is opaque and flakes, it's done. If it looks underdone, then replace the lid, turn the heat to high and steam for an additional 5 minutes.

■ When done, take the dish out of the steamer and set it on a heatproof surface. Place your serving platter next to the fish. Using the parchment, lift the fish out of the steamer dish and place on the serving platter. Shimmy the parchment out from under the fish. Then pour the sauce mixture evenly over the fish. Garnish with cilantro and serve.

MOM SAYS: If you're going to steam a whole fish, be sure you have a big enough steamer to accommodate it. Measure the diameter of the steamer before you go to the seafood shop. And if your steamer isn't big enough for a whole fish, you can use fish fillets. While serving whole fish is symbolic at Lunar New Year, if you can't, you can't. Sometimes you have to lean into the spirit if not the letter of the tradition.

陰
曆
新
年

Winter melon is symbolic of growth and good health. It's usually candied and comes as part of a "togetherness" candy tray, but the candy can be cloying, so this soup is another way to enjoy winter melon, which is actually a gourd. Making this soup couldn't be easier—with just a few ingredients and water. If you have good chicken or vegetable broth, use that instead. One of our favorite ways to make this soup is with a smoked ham hock, which creates loads of flavor. Asian markets tend to sell winter melon cut into large segments, because the whole gourd is rather large.

冬瓜湯 (素)

WINTER MELON SOUP

EFFORT ●○○

MAKES 4 TO 6 SERVINGS, FAMILY STYLE

1 large chunk of winter melon (about 3 pounds)

6 cups Chinese-Style Chicken Broth (page 226) or vegetable broth or water

2 small slices fresh ginger, about ¼ inch thick and 1 inch long

1 green onion, cut into 2-inch segments

1 tablespoon soy sauce

1 tablespoon Shaoxing wine (optional)

1 teaspoon kosher salt, plus more as needed

■ Cut the winter melon into several pieces. Then trim off the rind and cut out the seeds (or scrape them off with a spoon). Cut the melon pieces into 2-inch chunks. They don't have to be even, but you don't want chunks that are too small—when cooked too long, the flesh breaks down and "melts."

■ Combine the winter melon, broth or water, ginger, green onion, soy sauce, and wine in a large soup pot. Bring the mixture to a boil, then turn the heat to low. Let simmer for 20 to 25 minutes, or until the winter melon is tender. Add 1 teaspoon salt and taste for seasoning. If needed, add more salt to taste. Serve.

MOM SAYS: When you use water to make this recipe, you get a more subtle flavor than you would if you use broth. It's an opportunity for you to calm down your palate and learn how to appreciate gentler flavors.

Snow peas represent unity—and the bright-green color reminds us of spring. This dish could work with a range of proteins, including chicken, pork, shrimp, and scallops (which are delicate and need a tender touch). You could even combine proteins, such as chicken and scallops or shrimp and scallops. We chose beef because at Lunar New Year, you want to have a little bit of everything from land and sea to show abundance.

雪豆牛肉 (海鮮醬口味)
HOISIN BEEF
with Snow Peas

EFFORT ●○○

**MAKES 4 SERVINGS,
FAMILY STYLE**

8 ounces flank steak

2 tablespoons soy sauce, divided

2 teaspoons cornstarch

4 ounces snow peas

2½ tablespoons hoisin sauce

1 tablespoon water

1 teaspoon grated fresh ginger

1 teaspoon crushed or finely minced garlic

1½ tablespoons vegetable oil, divided

½ teaspoon freshly ground black pepper

■ Trim the flank steak of any large pieces of membrane. Cut the flank in half or thirds lengthwise, or with the grain. Depending on the total width of the flank, you may get two or three sections that are about 3 inches wide. Cut these sections against the grain into ⅛-inch slices. Place the beef in a medium bowl. Add 1 tablespoon of the soy sauce and mix well. Then add the cornstarch and mix well again. Set aside.

■ To trim the snow peas, pick off the stem. If there's a little brown "tail" on the opposite end of the pod, pick that off too. Repeat for all the snow peas. Set aside. In a small bowl, combine the remaining 1 tablespoon soy sauce with the hoisin, water, ginger, and garlic. Stir to combine. Set aside.

■ Preheat a wok over high heat until wisps of smoke rise from the surface. Swirl in 1 tablespoon of the vegetable oil and heat until it starts to shimmer. Gently add the beef and, using a wok spatula, spread it into a single layer. Sear for about 30 seconds and then stir-fry for 1 to 2 minutes, or until the meat has browned. It's okay if there are some pieces that are undercooked. Turn off the heat and transfer the beef back to the same bowl. Set aside.

■ Scrape off any bits and pieces on the surface of the wok. If needed, give it a light scrub and rinse in the sink, being mindful that the wok is still very hot. Return the wok to high heat. Swirl in the remaining ½ tablespoon vegetable oil. Let heat for about 10 seconds. Add the snow peas and stir-fry for about 30 seconds. Add the beef and stir-fry for about 1 minute. Swirl in the sauce mixture and stir-fry for another minute. Sprinkle with the black pepper and stir again. Turn off the heat and transfer to a serving dish.

MOM SAYS: This dish would work just as well with sugar snap peas, though you may want to slice the pods into bite-size segments.

Lantern Festival

Fifteenth Day, First Month

LANTERN FESTIVAL RECIPES

元
宵
節

WHAT'S LANTERN FESTIVAL?

元宵節快樂!
Yuánxiāo jié kuàilè!
Happy Lantern Festival!

Worshipping the moon is a theme for many holidays, and the Mandarin name for Lantern Festival, Yuánxiāo Jié, represents the night of the first full moon of the year. It's when people eat tang yuan—glutinous rice balls—that have sweet or savory fillings. Red bean, black sesame, and chestnut are popular sweet flavors. Also called yuán xiāo, tang yuan have a round shape that mimics the fullness of the moon and symbolizes the circle of family and wishes for a peaceful life. Tang yuan have a sticky, slightly chewy shell, and when you bite into them, the filling oozes out like lava. You cook them in water that gains body as the dumplings release some of their starch. This becomes the "broth" that you ladle into a bowl with a few tang yuan. It's not a soup but it's a soup. It's hard to eat more than a few of these because they are rich.

Since Lantern Festival caps the two-week celebration of Lunar New Year, people are already in a festive mood. Families have been gathering together and feasting. It's fitting that

幸
福
饗
宴

tang yuan bring a bit of sweetness to wrap up the festivities. Also, after the Lantern Festival, all the superstitions (such as not cutting your hair lest you cut your good luck) that go into effect during the Lunar New Year celebration end.

One of the traditions that began during the Southern Song dynasty (1127–1279) is the writing of riddles on pieces of paper and affixing them to the lanterns. Then, as everyone is strolling the neighborhood to admire the lanterns, they stop to read the riddles and try to solve them. Young couples take this opportunity to spend time together too, so Lantern Festival is also known as Chinese Valentine's Day. Lighting the lanterns represents reconciliation, forgiveness, and letting go of the previous year in order to light a path to a fortuitous new year.

There are numerous legends about the origins of the Lantern Festival. One relates to the Jade Emperor, who was the ruler of heaven, and whose favorite crane flew down to Earth and was mistaken for a regular bird. A villager killed the crane, not knowing it belonged to the Jade Emperor, who was furious and planned to burn down the village. Versions of this story say it was the emperor's daughter or godmother or a wise old man who warned the villagers of impending doom and advised them to hang red lanterns and set off firecrackers to make it appear as if the village was burning down. It was enough to trick the Jade Emperor into thinking the village was burning down so he didn't have to do it himself.

Another origin tale describes how an emperor during the Han dynasty (206 BCE to 220 CE) noticed that the Buddhist monks would light lanterns on the fifteenth day of the first month to honor Buddha and decreed that everyone in the kingdom would also light lanterns. Yet another tale describes a maid named Yuán-Xiāo who worked at the palace and was sad she couldn't visit her family. One of the emperor's advisers took pity on the maid and created an elaborate ruse that eventually led her to make glutinous rice balls and reunite with her family. Because Yuán-Xiāo's glutinous rice balls were the best, they were named yuán xiāo after her.

While you can make your own tang yuan or yuán xiāo—the name difference also reflects stylistic differences in how they're filled and shaped—you also can buy them. Well-stocked Asian markets often have long freezer cases stocked with multiple brands and styles of tang yuan. They definitely require less effort and you can try as many flavors as you'd like.

Red Bean Tang Yuan (page 87) filling process.

MEILEE'S PERSPECTIVE: A LETTER FROM A PICKY EATER

Dear Parents, Teens,
or Whoever May Read This:

We should talk. You, the adventurers of food and culinary wonders, and me, your favorite picky eater of today. It's unlikely that we would get along, right? Wrong. I am here today on a quest of my own, to bridge generations and cultures and, right now (and most importantly), taste buds.

And in the spirit of the Lantern Festival, when people let go of the past and light the way forward, I wanted to talk about my rocky relationship with food.

Many kids my age can sympathize, I'm sure, with struggling with new flavors and textures. While the many adults in my life have enjoyed the complex collection of flavors spread across their tables, I have often found comfort in the familiarity of plain dishes. Whether it be stir-fried chicken or even just a bowl of white rice, I am okay with simple and repetitive flavors.

Everyone has their "thing" when it comes to pickiness of food. Take my brother, for example: he takes the filling out of dumplings and prefers to eat just the wrapper. My lau lau will eat any meat down to the bare bone, except for lamb. My dad really doesn't like brussels sprouts. My mom can't stand raw onions. What I am trying to get at is, it's okay to not like things. I know getting the title of "picky eater" is more than just not liking a few things, but it is important that you remember that.

I have always struggled with trying new foods. Growing up, it was simply because I didn't want to branch out, and, later in life, it was because of recovering from my eating disorder. Whatever the reason, you could not get me to try a new food if my life depended on it. I am proud to say that has recently started to change. I got a job as a server's assistant in October of 2022 at the local Seattle restaurant Brimmer & Heeltap. Working in the restaurant business was intimidating at first. It was a lot of new rules, new perspectives, and a lot of new foods. If I ever wanted to be able to serve food and take orders, I needed to learn the menu and try new foods. So I swallowed whatever fear I had and I did it. I always took a bite of whatever someone asked me to try. Sure, I didn't always like what I tried, and I didn't go out of my way to try new foods either, but the point is I did it.

My advice to anyone who struggles with food is to remember you don't need to like everything, but there is no harm in trying. Believe me, I know that is easier said than done, but I know you can do it. I am doing my best to follow that, but it doesn't always go as planned, and that is okay. Your adventures with food are yours and do not need to follow any criteria or rubric. I hope you can recognize that although our ventures in food are different, they are not obstacles but bridges. Bridges that span time and culture, bringing us closer despite whatever may separate us.

So, if you are a picky eater, I hope that you will have heard my story and will now embark on a food adventure of your own with an open heart and a willing palate, ready to savor the past and embrace the future. Thank you for taking the time to hear me out. This letter marks where I was, the things I am learning, and I hope soon enough you'll see where I am headed. I promise to carry your legacy of adventurous eating forward.

Keep eating,

PS: You may be wondering why I am a part of this book. All my life, I've wanted a relatable form of media, something that even somewhat represented me. So when my mom came to me and asked if I wanted to write this book with her, I knew that I should do it. My mom wanted me to help bridge the generation gap and get young people engaged about their culture and excited to cook. I am really excited that I get to do that with my writing in this book.

幸
福
饗
宴

湯圓麵團
TANG YUAN DOUGH

VEGAN

EFFORT ●○○

MAKES ENOUGH DOUGH FOR 12 LARGE OR 24 SMALL TANG YUAN

1 cup sweet rice flour (glutinous rice flour)

½ cup warm water (about 110 degrees F)

It's important to get sweet rice flour, which is also known as glutinous rice flour, to make this dough. Regular rice flour won't work. You likely will have to go to an Asian market or buy it online. That said, Mochiko sweet rice flour from Koda Farms is widely available.

■ In a medium bowl, combine the sweet rice flour with the water. Stir together until bits of dough start to form. Then use your hand to gather the shards together into a ball of dough. Keep kneading the dough for a few minutes until it's smooth and holds together. Cover the dough to keep it from drying out. Use this dough to make tang yuan with your choice of filling and cook according to instructions (see recipes in this chapter).

MOM SAYS: In case you're wondering, a stand mixer doesn't really help when making such a small quantity of dough, especially if you have a large-capacity work bowl like I do.

Red bean paste is sweet and spreadable—our version of peanut butter or Nutella. You can find red bean paste in different consistencies from chunky to smooth. We prefer the smooth red bean paste for this filling because the tang yuan are so small. Having chunks of red bean might puncture the dough. You will have leftover red bean paste that you can use for other purposes.

■ Set out a dinner plate lined with parchment paper. Roll the dough into a rope about 12 inches long and cut into twelve pieces. Take one piece of dough and roll it a few times until it's a smooth ball. Press the ball gently between your palms to flatten into a disk. Using your fingers and thumbs, press the disk into a small bowl shape. Place about 1 teaspoon of the red bean paste in the middle of the dough. If you get any filling on your fingers, wipe them clean before the next step. Carefully gather the dough around the filling and pinch it closed. Once the filling has been sealed inside the dough, roll the ball between your palms to smooth out the edges. Set the ball on the parchment-lined plate. Repeat with the remaining pieces of dough.

■ Add 4 cups of water to a small pot. Bring to a boil over high heat. Add the tang yuan carefully. They will fall to the bottom. It's important to use a cooking spoon or rubber spatula to gently nudge them off the bottom of the pot. Let them cook for 5 to 8 minutes, or until they float and the dough starts to look translucent. Serve the tang yuan in small bowls with some of the cooking liquid.

> **MOM SAYS:** If you want, you can make bigger batches to freeze. Place the uncooked tang yuan on a small baking sheet lined with parchment paper. Freeze them for several hours and then transfer them to a ziplock bag. Cook frozen ones for 8 to 10 minutes. By the way, red bean paste spread on sliced white bread was one of my favorite childhood snacks. I never had peanut butter and jelly sandwiches, but I had plenty of red bean paste sandwiches!

紅豆湯圓
RED BEAN TANG YUAN

VEGAN

EFFORT ●●○

MAKES 12 TANG YUAN

1 batch Tang Yuan Dough (page 86)

1 package (about 10 ounces) red bean paste, chilled

幸
福
饗
宴

黑芝麻湯圓
BLACK SESAME TANG YUAN

VEGETARIAN
EFFORT ●●○
MAKES 12 TANG YUAN

½ cup plus 2 tablespoons black sesame powder

5 to 6 tablespoons honey

1 batch Tang Yuan Dough (page 86)

Black sesame contains antioxidants and minerals and is thought to remedy hair loss. (Though if you eat too much, you'll experience one of its other functions—as a laxative.) To make the sweetened filling for tang yuan, you can use black sesame powder, which is more convenient than starting from the black sesame seeds themselves.

■ Combine the black sesame powder and honey in a small bowl. Stir to combine. When it gets thick and hard to stir, you can use a spatula to help press the powder and honey together. It will dry like glue, so be sure to cover the bowl when not actively using it.

■ Set out a dinner plate lined with parchment paper. Roll the dough into a rope about 12 inches long and cut into twelve pieces. Take one piece of dough and roll it a few times until it's a smooth ball. Press the ball gently between your palms to flatten into a disk. Using your fingers and thumbs, press the disk into a small bowl shape. Place about 1 teaspoon of the black sesame paste in the middle of the dough. If you get any filling on your fingers, wipe them clean before the next step. Carefully gather the dough around the filling and pinch it closed. Once the filling has been sealed inside the dough, roll the ball between your palms to smooth out the edges. Set the ball on the parchment-lined plate. Repeat with the remaining pieces of dough.

■ Add 4 cups of water to a small pot. Bring to a boil over high heat. Add the tang yuan carefully. They will fall to the bottom. It's important to use a cooking spoon or rubber spatula to gently nudge them off the bottom of the pot. Let them cook for 5 to 8 minutes, or until they float and the dough starts to look translucent. Serve the tang yuan in small bowls with some of the cooking liquid.

MOM SAYS: Be mindful of your first bite of this tang yuan. It will unleash black lava onto your tongue.

幸
福
饗
宴

雞肉蘑菇湯圓
CHICKEN AND MUSHROOM TANG YUAN

EFFORT ●●○
MAKES 12 TANG YUAN

8 ounces ground chicken

3 medium dried shiitake mushrooms, soaked for 2 to 3 hours in warm water, then very finely minced

2 tablespoons soy sauce

1 green onion, finely chopped

1 teaspoon finely minced fresh ginger

¼ teaspoon sesame oil

2 teaspoons cornstarch

1 batch Tang Yuan Dough (page 86)

This chicken filling is similar to what we use for making wonton soup. You could use different mushrooms and/or add cilantro to change it up. We haven't tried this with turkey (because we're not fans of turkey), but when we talk about ground chicken, people always ask about turkey. Yes, you can use turkey if you'd like. You will have leftover filling, which you can freeze to use later, or you can shape the rest into a patty and cook it in a skillet.

■ In a medium bowl, combine the ground chicken, mushrooms, soy sauce, green onions, ginger, and sesame oil. Mix well. Add the cornstarch and mix well again. Set aside.

■ Set out a dinner plate lined with parchment paper. Roll the dough into a rope about 12 inches long and cut into twelve pieces. Take one piece of dough and roll it a few times until it's a smooth ball. Press the ball gently between your palms to flatten into a disk. Using your fingers and thumbs, press the disk into a small bowl shape. Place about 1 teaspoon of the filling in the middle of the dough. If you get any filling on your fingers, wipe them clean before the next step. Carefully gather the dough around the filling and pinch it closed. Once the filling has been sealed inside the dough, roll the ball between your palms to smooth out the edges. Set the ball on the parchment-lined plate. Repeat with the remaining pieces of dough.

■ Add 4 cups of water to a small pot. Bring to a boil over high heat. Add the tang yuan carefully. They will fall to the bottom. It's important to use a cooking spoon or rubber spatula to gently nudge them off the bottom of the pot. Let them cook for 6 to 8 minutes, or until they float and the dough starts to look translucent. Serve the tang yuan in small bowls with some of the cooking liquid.

MOM SAYS: You could also serve these tang yuan in Chinese-Style Chicken Broth (page 226).

Chinese chives are like an intense mash-up of green onions and garlic. They pair well with pork, which is a combination that also shows up in jiaozi (dumplings). You can play with the amount of chives if you prefer a more pungent flavor. You will have leftover filling, which you can freeze to use later, or you can shape the rest into a patty and cook it in a skillet.

■ In a medium bowl, combine the ground pork, chives, soy sauce, green onions, ginger, and sesame oil. Mix well. Add the cornstarch and mix well again. Set aside.

■ Set out a dinner plate lined with parchment paper. Roll the dough into a rope about 12 inches long and cut into twelve pieces. Take one piece of dough and roll it a few times until it's a smooth ball. Press the ball gently between your palms to flatten into a disk. Using your fingers and thumbs, press the disk into a small bowl shape. Place about 1 teaspoon of the filling in the middle of the dough. If you get any filling on your fingers, wipe them clean before the next step. Carefully gather the dough around the filling and pinch it closed. Once the filling has been sealed inside the dough, roll the ball between your palms to smooth out the edges. Set the ball on the parchment-lined plate. Repeat with the remaining pieces of dough.

■ Add 4 cups of water to a small pot. Bring to a boil over high heat. Add the tang yuan carefully. They will fall to the bottom. It's important to use a cooking spoon or rubber spatula to gently nudge them off the bottom of the pot. Let them cook for 6 to 8 minutes, or until they float and the dough starts to look translucent. Serve the tang yuan in small bowls with some of the cooking liquid.

> **MOM SAYS:** If you want to add another dimension to the flavor profile, you can mince some kimchi and add it to the pork mixture.

韭菜豬肉湯圓
PORK AND CHINESE CHIVES TANG YUAN

EFFORT ●●○
MAKES 12 TANG YUAN

8 ounces ground pork

½ cup finely chopped Chinese chives

2 tablespoons soy sauce

1 green onion, finely chopped

1 teaspoon finely minced fresh ginger

¼ teaspoon sesame oil

2 teaspoons cornstarch

1 batch Tang Yuan Dough (page 86)

Qingming Festival

Fifth Day, Fourth Month

QINGMING FESTIVAL RECIPES

WHAT'S QINGMING FESTIVAL?

清明平安

qīng míng píng ān

Wishing you peace during the Qingming Festival

Qingming is Tomb-Sweeping Day to honor the dead. Families visit the graves of loved ones, clean up around the tombs, make food offerings, and burn incense and fake money—or ghost money—to send to the afterlife. It's said that the reason there's a dedicated day for tomb-sweeping is because in ancient China, there were so many formal ceremonies to honor ancestors or mark holidays that it became too costly. Tang dynasty emperor Xuanzong proclaimed in 732 CE that people would pay tribute to ancestors only during Qingming, thereby reducing the frequency and expense of these ceremonies. Because the holiday takes place on or around April 5, when the weather is becoming more pleasant, families also will have picnics or spend time outdoors.

This duty to honor ancestors stems from the Confucian belief in filial piety. It's about demonstrating proper respect and love to your parents, elders, and forebears. It guides formal behaviors and practices and the use of honorifics. Parents describe good children as xiào shùn (孝顺), meaning "respect and obedience."

Qingming is also called Pure Brightness Day, which is based on the legend of Jie Zitui from the seventh century BCE. Jie Zitui was a loyal minister to Prince Chong Er, who was exiled from his home state of Jin for nineteen years. During a lean period, Jie Zitui even sacrificed a piece of flesh from his own leg to make soup to feed the prince, which saved his life. After the prince was able to return home and assume his title as a duke, he rewarded all those who had served him in exile except for Jie Zitui, whom he had forgotten. Jie Zitui then left for the mountains with his mother.

When the duke recognized his error, he searched for Jie Zitui in the mountains. When they couldn't find him amid the dense forest, they burned it down in hopes of smoking him out. Instead, they found that Jie Zitui and his mother had died under a willow tree. Before he perished, he wrote and stuffed a letter in the tree. It stated that he remained loyal and that he hoped to be remembered for being pure and bright. In Jie Zitui's honor, the duke proclaimed the day to be called Hanshi Festival and that there would be no fires allowed anywhere. So, on the day of the Hanshi Festival, only cold food could be had. And the next day would be the Pure Brightness Day. While folks don't celebrate Hanshi Festival now, having cold foods on Pure Brightness Day or Qingming endures.

In contemporary times, the reason people tomb sweep only once a year is not just because of the official holiday. According to a study conducted in Taiwan and published in *Landscape Research* in 2007, people don't go to cemeteries the rest of the year because the landscape is a mess. A lack of planning and oversight led to crowded, overgrown cemeteries with tombstones in disarray due to feng shui practices. Crowded cemeteries are a widespread issue across China and Taiwan, where burial plots are located on terraced mountainsides. *The Guardian* published a stunning collection of photos of cemeteries in Hong Kong in 2015. It's hard to fathom how these cemeteries were built and the amount of human labor necessary to transport tombstones to these plots.

And during Qingming, or anytime one needs to make the trek to pay respect to their forebears, people arrive with fruit baskets and little containers of snacks and other foods to place on the tombs.

Mom Says

This chapter is dedicated to my father, Chang-Sheng Chou, who passed away in 2005. His name means "long life," but he lived only to the age of sixty-three. All the recipes that follow represent some of his favorite foods and aren't specifically connected to Qingming. He loved to eat and, while he was a principled man, he didn't have the discipline to refrain from the carb- and sugar-laden foods that were detrimental to his health as a diabetic.

My father didn't like to talk about the scarcity he experienced growing up, but it drove his generosity when it came to feeding people and making sure others had enough. It also, perhaps, altered his synapses and heightened his desire to eat what he wanted, like the canned-dessert congee or sweetened grass jelly or too much white rice and, and, and. The root of it was in a recurring memory my father would share when the mood struck: before my uncle—my father's older brother—left for the military, he said, "Let's go eat a full meal."

It always broke my heart to hear that story, because it was a shorthand between two brothers who had grown up lacking many basic necessities. "I couldn't even afford the few dollars for a pair of gym shorts and had to borrow them from my classmates," my father would recall about those days. "Your yeh yeh (grandpa) was always served first and got the best cuts at the dinner table."

We immigrated to the United States in 1974, when I was two. It was not easy for my father to leave his mother in Taipei. She was illiterate and had had her feet bound when she was young, which caused her many difficulties as she aged. My parents had the opportunity to come to the United States and scraped—and I mean *scraped*—together the funds for the paperwork and the travel expenses. My father was studying for a master's in journalism. He would wait tables in the summer and between semesters to send money back to his mother. "Yeh Yeh did not treat your nai nai (grandma), well," he said. "Nai Nai loved you most. She cried and cried when we told her we were coming to the US."

Heartbreak came in 1979 with the news that my grandmother had died. Because of our visa status, my father could not leave the country to attend her funeral. If he had, he would not have been able to return. It would take several more years before we would finally receive our green cards. The very first trip we took was back to Taipei.

There are three times I can recall seeing my father sob openly: when my grandmother died, the first trip back to Taipei to visit her grave, and the last trip back to visit her grave. By the time the last trip took place in the spring of 2004, my father was ailing from complications due to his diabetes and several strokes. He required a walker or a wheelchair and was on dialysis. He had been settling his affairs over the course of a couple of years, which included making good on the promise to take my mother back to Paris to have a cup of coffee on the Champs-Elysées and to make this final visit to his mother's grave. I had the honor of going with him and my mother.

The cemeteries on mountainsides are no joke and are definitely not accessible for anyone with mobility issues. Getting to Nai Nai's grave required descending one hundred stone steps, which were twice as brutal on the return climb. With my uncle leading the way, my father hugged the railing as he hobbled painfully down the stairs. We brought Nai Nai the biggest sweet peaches we could find at the nearby wet market—they weren't the local honey peaches, though, that my father would dream about and preferred, because it was too early in the season. We prostrated ourselves before Nai Nai's tomb, my father paying his respects to his mother for what he knew would be the last time. Then he used every ounce of regret and sorrow for not being able to be at her side when she died to will his legs up one hundred stone steps and out of anguish. Back in the car, he thanked me for accompanying him and lending my knee as a stool when he needed to rest on the uphill hike. How could I not? I was Nai Nai's favorite, after all.

MEILEE'S PERSPECTIVE: A CONVERSATION WITH MY LAU LAU ABOUT MY GRANDFATHER

I have never experienced the death of a loved one. My grandfather on my mom's side died before I was born. Growing up, we were told all kinds of stories about him, that he was stern but caring. He was a very hard worker and did everything he could to support his family. A picture of him sits on a shelf in the living room. It serves not only as a reminder of him but also feels like a portal so he can watch over our lives. I wanted to learn more about him, so I decided to talk to my lau lau (his wife).

Q: How did you two meet?

LAU LAU: We were in the same class when we were in the military academy. We were both majoring in journalism.

Q: What was he like?

LAU LAU: He was skinnier than our other classmates. He was always studying very hard and he was known as "the walking dictionary." He liked my Chinese writing. The head of our department assigned us one article to write each week, whatever style, just to practice our writing skills. So I submitted all different kinds of styles of writing, and it always ended up being published in the school paper. He concentrated on studying everything, especially English. He kept a dictionary with all of his notes (laughter). We developed in different directions.

Q: How do you think he would react if he met all of us (the seven grandkids)?

LAU LAU: Well, he only met Jackson when Jackson was very small. But he got to enjoy everything about being a grandpa, because Jackson already knew how to say, "Yeh Yeh." So he would always climb the stairs and say "Yeh Yeh!" One time, Jackson climbed in his bed and used the shaver and tried to shave him. (More laughter.) He enjoyed grandkids, but he got so sick (and died) and he couldn't enjoy all of you.

Q: What do you miss about him?

LAU LAU: Well (pointing to a picture of him displayed under her computer and laughing), he was very caring. He cared a lot about his mother and me and Hsiao-Ching and all the kids. He taught your uncle Sam about Chinese history. At night, Uncle Sam would give him a massage and during that time when they were together, he always taught him about Chinese history and all that. And so that's their father-and-son togetherness. He expected more from Hsiao-Ching, because he wanted her to build a strong inside. Instead of pursuing all the outside glory, he wanted her to build up a very strong character and study and

develop a strong power of knowledge and abilities. Uncle Dave was very young when my husband found out he had a serious kidney problem. So Uncle Sam and your mom helped to bring up their younger brother. So before he died, he was holding the three of them together and he said: "Take care of your mom. The three of you need to bond together and take care of your mom." And those were his last words.

The topic of the afterlife is something I've never really delved into. I wasn't raised with any particular religious beliefs, so heaven and hell have always seemed a bit foreign to me. However, one thing I'm sure of is that I hope for my grandfather to have found peace, wherever he may be now. My hope is that he's watching over us, especially as my cousins and I grow up to become the strong, intelligent, and kind individuals he would have wanted us to be.

幸
福
饗
宴

水果盤
FRUIT PLATTER

VEGAN

EFFORT ●○○

MAKES 4 SERVINGS, FAMILY STYLE

When bringing a fruit offering for tomb-sweeping, it's usually simple: a few perfect peaches, a small bunch of lychee, a few tangerines, or something that the ancestor liked. If we're honoring a loved one at the table with a meal, then we put together a platter of cut fruit. That's the ultimate show of care. You can use whatever fruit you like and what's delicious in your area during a given season. Cut the fruit and arrange on a pretty platter. Here are some ideas for groupings of fruit by season or by type.

FALL/WINTER
1 large Asian pear, such as
20th Century
2 persimmons
1 pomelo
1 large star fruit

TROPICAL
1 mango
1 dragon fruit
1 papaya
1 small bunch lychees
2 passion fruits

SIMPLE
2 navel oranges
1 bunch grapes

SUMMER
Watermelon
Honeydew
Cantaloupe
Pineapple

STONE FRUITS
2 peaches
1 nectarine
3 plums
Cherries

MOM SAYS: When you're preparing the fruit, make sure your cutting board and knife are clean. You don't want to cut fruit on the same board that you've just used for cutting onions or raw proteins, for example. One of my peeves is expecting to taste the fruit but getting an onion taste instead. It doesn't matter so much, however, when you're cutting fruit for a savory dish.

清
明
節

Scallion pancakes make great wraps for any number of fillings. We've stuffed them with grilled lemongrass pork, vegetable stir-fry, and whatever ingredients needed a savory, chewy canvas. If you're at the Chinese barbecue shop to get duck, you might as well pick up some barbecue pork or chicken. Those would also taste delicious in the pancake. While the recipe calls for half a duck, you can buy a whole duck so that you have extras to eat or to make soup (page 149). Ask the chef not to chop up the duck so that you can shred the meat.

烤鴨蔥油捲餅
SCALLION PANCAKE ROLLS
with Chinese Barbecue Duck

EFFORT ●●○

MAKES 4 SERVINGS AS AN APPETIZER

2½ cups unbleached all-purpose flour, plus more for dusting

¾ cup warm water (95 to 100 degrees F)

½ Chinese barbecue duck; keep the duck half intact, not chopped

6 tablespoons vegetable oil, divided

1½ teaspoons kosher salt, divided, plus more as needed

4 green onions, finely chopped

4 to 6 tablespoons hoisin sauce, divided

2 Persian cucumbers (or the small "cocktail cucumber"), sliced into paper-thin slices

½ cup finely chopped fresh cilantro, divided

Chili crisp or other hot sauce (optional)

■ To make the dough, place the flour in a mixing bowl. Add the water and, using a rubber spatula or wooden spoon, stir the water and flour together. Continue to stir gently until a ball of dough starts to form. Start kneading the dough to make a ball. The dough should feel slightly tacky but not damp. Cover the dough with a damp towel or plastic wrap and let it rest for a minimum of 20 minutes and up to several hours.

■ Meanwhile, using a paring knife, a fork, and/or your fingers, remove the duck meat from the carcass. You want large shreds or carved slices of the duck meat. Be sure to include pieces of the skin (see note). Place the duck pieces on a plate. Set aside.

■ Set up the assembly line for the onion pancakes. Place 2 tablespoons of the vegetable oil in a small bowl and set a small pastry brush next to it. In another small dish, place the 1½ teaspoons of kosher salt. Set the chopped green onions in a small bowl next to the salt.

■ Divide the dough in half. Lightly dust your work surface. Roll one piece of dough out to about 10 inches in diameter. Brush a coating of oil onto the dough. Sprinkle about ¾ teaspoon salt across the oiled dough, making sure to sprinkle from a height of 8 to 10 inches above the dough. This helps to distribute the salt more evenly across the surface.

■ Spread 3 tablespoons or so of green onions across the dough. Starting from the bottom edge of the round of dough, roll the dough tightly into a tube. Then take one end of the tube and coil it into a tightly wound coil. Gently stretch and tuck the end under the coil. Roll the coiled dough flat until it's about 11½ inches in diameter and about ⅛ inch thick. Repeat with the other piece of dough. ⟶

■ Preheat a 12-inch skillet over medium-low heat for about 1 minute. Add 3 tablespoons of oil and heat for about 5 seconds, or until it starts to shimmer. Add a pancake and fry for 1½ to 2 minutes on each side, or until golden. Remove the pancake and set aside on a plate lined with paper towels to absorb any excess oil. Add the remaining 1 tablespoon oil to the pan before cooking the other pancake.

■ To make the rolls: Place one pancake before you. Spread 2 tablespoons of the hoisin sauce onto the pancake. Add slices of cucumber, spreading them throughout but without completely covering up the hoisin sauce. Spread out bits of duck and skin. Garnish with half the cilantro leaves. Drizzle on some chili crisp to taste. Starting from the bottom edge, roll the pancake up. If needed, use toothpicks to hold the roll together. Slice in half. Repeat with the other pancake. Serve as a snack or an appetizer.

MOM SAYS: There's usually a layer of fat under the duck skin. If that doesn't suit your taste, you don't have to eat it. I don't mind a little duck fat, but sometimes the fat layer is overwhelming. So include or don't include the duck skin and fat in the roll; it's up to you.

Steamed spinach dumplings were a particular favorite of our late patriarch (Hsiao-Ching's father, who died in 2005). While he was an omnivore, he loved the lightness of the vegetable filling. The shiitake, onions, and seasoning help balance the astringency of the spinach.

■ In a medium bowl, combine all the ingredients, except the dumpling wrappers. Mix thoroughly.

■ Set up your dumpling-making station with the filling, stack of wrappers, and a small dish with about ¼ cup water. Line a baking sheet with parchment paper and set aside.

■ To make the dumplings, dip your index finger in the water and brush the outer edge of the wrapper. Repeat until the outer edge is moistened. Place 1 heaping teaspoon of the filling in the center of the wrapper. Fold the wrapper over the filling into a half-moon shape. Match the edges together and press as if you were sealing an envelope. Holding the sealed edge of the dumpling between your fingers, set it on its spine and gently wiggle it as you push down so that the dumpling will stand up. Place the completed dumpling on the parchment-lined baking sheet. Repeat to prepare the remaining dumplings.

■ To cook, set up your steamer (see page 37). Line the steamer basket with perforated parchment. Place the dumplings in the basket, leaving about ¾ inch between dumplings. In batches, steam over high heat for 8 to 10 minutes, or until the wrappers are translucent. Serve with Dumpling Dipping Sauce, chili crisp, or your favorite sauce.

MOM SAYS: If you want to double down on the spinach, you can look for green dumpling wrappers. You'll most likely have to go to an Asian market to find spinach-infused wrappers.

素蒸菠菜餃
STEAMED SPINACH DUMPLINGS

VEGAN
EFFORT ●●●
MAKES 30 TO 35 DUMPLINGS

2 green onions, finely chopped

1 (10-ounce) package of frozen cut spinach, defrosted (speed this up by soaking in warm water and then straining well, gently squeezing out the excess water)

1 cup grated carrot

½ cup diced fresh or rehydrated shiitake

2 tablespoons soy sauce

½ teaspoon grated fresh ginger

½ teaspoon sesame oil

⅛ teaspoon white pepper powder

1 package round dumpling wrappers (also called gyoza wrappers)

Dumpling Dipping Sauce (page 58) or chili crisp, for serving

幸
福
饗
宴

素菜燒豆腐
BRAISED TOFU
with Vegetables

EFFORT ●○○

MAKES 4 TO 6 SERVINGS, FAMILY STYLE

4 cups Chinese-Style Chicken Broth (page 226) or water

2 cups Chinese cabbage, sliced roughly into 1-inch squares

8 small dried shiitake mushrooms, soaked in warm water for 2 to 3 hours

3 slices ginger coins, about ¼ inch thick and 1 inch wide

1 small carrot, sliced ¼ inch thick

1 green onion, cut into 2-inch segments

1 tablespoon soy sauce

About 7 ounces soft tofu, cut into ½-inch-thick slabs

1 teaspoon kosher salt, plus more as needed

8 snow peas, trimmed

1 bundle bean thread, soaked in warm water

This dish is intentionally low-key and made for days when you need warmth and gentleness. The combination of vegetables is flexible. You can use different mushrooms or a combination of mushrooms. Just remember to leave quick-cooking ingredients like snow peas or bean thread till the end.

■ In a medium soup pot, combine the broth, cabbage, mushrooms, ginger, carrots, green onions, and soy sauce. Bring to a boil over high heat. Reduce the heat to medium-low and let simmer for 10 to 15 minutes. Add the tofu, very carefully stirring to combine. Let simmer for another 10 minutes. Taste for seasoning and add 1 teaspoon salt or more to taste. Add the snow peas and the bean thread. Once the bean thread is translucent, the soup is ready. Serve with rice.

MOM SAYS: One of the traditional vessels in which to cook a braise like this is a clay pot. Clay pots get very hot and retain heat, so the braise bubbles away at the table. If you decide to try using a clay pot, be sure to research how to use one and be extra careful about safe-handling. You do not want to get burned!

While this recipe is vegan, you can easily add protein to it. It would taste great with tofu, chicken, or beef. In-season asparagus tastes freshest and costs less. Don't forget to soak the dried shiitake in advance to rehydrate. Fresh shiitake would work well too. If the caps are smaller, leave them whole. For larger shiitake, consider slicing the caps in half.

素炒冬菇蘆筍
STIR-FRIED ASPARAGUS
with Shiitake Mushrooms

- Preheat a wok over high heat until wisps of smoke rise from the surface. Swirl in the vegetable oil and let heat for a few seconds until it starts to shimmer. Add the asparagus and stir-fry for about 1 minute. Add the mushrooms and stir-fry for about 1 minute. Add the soy sauce, water, garlic, and ginger, and stir to combine, about 1 minute. Drizzle with the sesame oil and add the white pepper. Give it one last toss, then remove from the heat and transfer to a serving dish. Serve with rice.

VEGAN
EFFORT ● ○ ○
MAKES 4 SERVINGS, FAMILY STYLE

2 teaspoons vegetable oil

1 pound fresh asparagus, cut into 1½-inch segments

8 small or 6 medium dried shiitake mushrooms, soaked in warm water for 2 hours or until rehydrated, or fresh shiitake

1 tablespoon soy sauce

1 tablespoon water

1 to 2 cloves garlic, crushed

½ teaspoon grated fresh ginger

½ teaspoon sesame oil

⅛ teaspoon white pepper powder

MOM SAYS: Asparagus stalks can vary in thickness. If the stalks are especially big, slice them on the bias ¼ inch thick so that they cook quickly and come in contact with the sauce.

幸
福
饗
宴

素菜炒米粉
RICE VERMICELLI
with Vegetables

VEGAN

EFFORT ●○○

MAKES 4 SERVINGS, FAMILY STYLE

1 tablespoon vegetable oil

2 green onions, finely chopped

½ medium carrot, peeled and cut into fine strips (about ½ cup) or thinly sliced into coins

1 stalk celery, sliced on the bias ⅛ inch thick

2 cups chopped baby bok choy

½ cup sliced mushrooms, such as shiitake or cremini, or use brown beech mushrooms

⅓ pound dried rice vermicelli noodles (also called rice stick), soaked in warm water for 20 minutes to soften

2 tablespoons soy sauce

2 tablespoons water

2 cloves garlic, crushed

½ teaspoon sesame oil

Keeping a package of dried rice vermicelli (also known as rice stick) in the pantry means that you can whip up this dish anytime. You can add any combination of vegetables and proteins to make this dish your own. Remember to cut the ingredients in similar shapes or sizes so that they cook evenly.

■ Preheat a wok over high heat until wisps of smoke rise from the surface. Swirl in the vegetable oil and let heat for a few seconds until it starts to shimmer. Add the green onions and stir-fry for about 10 seconds. Add the carrot and celery and stir-fry for about 30 seconds. Add the bok choy and mushrooms and stir-fry for about 1 minute. Reduce the heat to medium. Add the noodles and stir-fry for 1 minute to combine. Add the soy sauce, water, and garlic. Stir-fry for 1 to 2 minutes to combine thoroughly. Turn off the heat. Add the sesame oil, give it one last stir, then transfer to a serving dish.

MOM SAYS: If you have leftovers, you can add vegetable broth or Chinese-Style Chicken Broth (page 226) to this the next day and make a quick soup. Adjust the seasoning as needed. It's a great way to use up leftovers but have it feel like a fresh dish.

These meatballs are called lion's head because they're usually made to be gigantic. Here, we make them smaller so that they're easier to eat. While you typically serve this with other dishes as part of a bigger meal, it's perfectly acceptable to make this *the* meal. If you can get Kurobuta or other heirloom ground pork, you'll get even more flavorful meatballs.

迷你狮子頭
MINI LION'S HEAD MEATBALLS

EFFORT ● ○ ○

MAKES 12 MINI MEATBALLS WITH BROTH

1 pound fatty ground pork (or unseasoned bulk ground sausage)

1 large egg, beaten

2 tablespoons soy sauce

1 tablespoon cornstarch

1 teaspoon grated fresh ginger

2 green onions, finely chopped

Vegetable oil, for frying

8 ounces Chinese cabbage leaves, cut into roughly 3-inch pieces

4 cups water, plus more as needed

1 teaspoon kosher salt, plus more as needed

1 bundle bean thread (cellophane noodles)

■ In a large bowl, combine the ground pork, egg, soy sauce, cornstarch, ginger, and green onions. Mix thoroughly. Divide into 12 portions and roll each into a ball. Set aside on a parchment-lined baking sheet.

■ In a large, deep-sided skillet, add vegetable oil to a depth of 1 inch. Heat over medium heat to 350 degrees F.

■ Meanwhile, place the cabbage and water in a 6-quart or larger Dutch oven over medium heat.

■ When the oil is to temperature, carefully place the meatballs in the oil and fry for 1 to 2 minutes. Flip the meatballs and fry the other side for 1 to 2 minutes. Use a slotted spoon or tongs to carefully transfer the meatballs to the Dutch oven and nestle among the cabbage leaves. Raise the temperature to high and bring the liquid to a boil. Then reduce heat to low and let braise for about 45 minutes, or until the cabbage has cooked down to a creamy state. Check the liquid level occasionally and shift the meatballs as needed to keep them in the liquid. At about the 30-minute mark, taste the broth. Add 1 teaspoon salt or more to taste. About 10 minutes prior to serving, drop the bean thread into the broth and make sure it's submerged. It will cook quickly. Serve with rice.

MOM SAYS: Truth be told, I love the Chinese cabbage in this dish more than the meatballs themselves. It's one of my favorite ways to enjoy braised cabbage—in a meatball broth!

幸
福
饗
宴

毛豆炒蝦仁
STIR-FRIED EDAMAME
with Shrimp

EFFORT ●○○

MAKES 4 SERVINGS, FAMILY STYLE

12 ounces peeled and deveined shrimp (preferably size 26/30, though the size of shrimp is up to you and what's available)

1 teaspoon kosher salt, divided, plus more as needed

Egg white from 1 large egg

1 tablespoon cornstarch

2 tablespoons plus 1 teaspoon vegetable oil, divided

½ cup edamame (beans only, no pod)

¼ cup water

½ teaspoon sesame oil

⅛ teaspoon white pepper powder

People love to get a bowl of edamame when they go to a Japanese restaurant. Well, you can also stir-fry the beans themselves. If you buy frozen edamame in the pods, defrost them and then remove the beans from the shell before cooking. Sometimes, you can find shelled edamame, which is more convenient. These are not to be confused with frozen lima beans—which you also could use in this dish.

■ In a medium bowl, mix the shrimp with ½ teaspoon of the salt. Separate the egg white and yolk. Add the egg white to the shrimp. Save the egg yolk for another purpose or discard. Using a rubber spatula or a pair of chopsticks, mix the egg white and shrimp together well. Add the cornstarch and stir again to combine.

■ Preheat a wok over medium heat until wisps of smoke rise from the surface. Swirl in 2 tablespoons of the oil and let heat for a few seconds until the surface shimmers. Add the shrimp and spread into a single layer. Let sear for about 30 seconds, then flip and sear for another 30 seconds. Now actively stir-fry the shrimp for about 1 minute. Turn off the heat and transfer the shrimp to a clean bowl or plate and set aside.

■ Scrape out any bits that may have stuck to the surface of the wok or give the wok a quick scrub and rinse in the sink. It's very hot, so be careful. Dry off the surface with a towel. Return the wok to the stove over high heat. Immediately add the remaining 1 teaspoon vegetable oil and heat for a few seconds until the surface shimmers. Add the edamame and stir-fry for a few seconds. Add the shrimp, water, and the remaining ½ teaspoon salt. Stir-fry for about 1 minute. Add the sesame oil and white pepper. Give it one last toss and then turn off the heat. Carefully taste the sauce for seasoning, and if it needs a touch more salt, add a pinch to taste. Transfer to a serving dish. Serve with rice.

MOM SAYS: This recipe also works with frozen peas or a medley that contains peas, carrots, and corn. When in season, get fresh English peas from the farmers' market. Pop the peas out of the shells and use them in this dish. The freshness is incredible.

清
明
節

Salt-and-pepper shrimp is always a draw. Usually, the shrimp is in the shell and often with the head on. Part of the enjoyment is using your teeth and tongue to shimmy the shrimp out of the shell and sucking on the shell to get all the flavor, then discarding the shell remnants in a small pile on your plate. If fried well, it's possible to eat the shell too. The spice can come from white pepper or a mix of fresh chilies with green onions and garlic. Everyone has their own recipe. Here, we're using peeled shrimp to make it more crowd-friendly.

椒鹽蝦
EASY SALT-AND-PEPPER SHRIMP

EFFORT ● ● ○

MAKES 4 SERVINGS, FAMILY STYLE

1 teaspoon kosher salt, divided

¼ teaspoon white pepper powder

12 ounces peeled and deveined shrimp (ideally size 26/30, though the size of shrimp is up to you and what's available)

Egg white from 1 large egg

½ cup cornstarch

2 teaspoons vegetable oil, plus more for frying

2 green onions, finely chopped

4 cloves garlic, finely chopped

1 teaspoon finely minced fresh ginger

■ In a small bowl, stir together ½ teaspoon of the kosher salt and the white pepper. Set aside.

■ In a medium bowl, mix the shrimp with the remaining ½ teaspoon salt and the egg white. Using a rubber spatula or a pair of chopsticks, mix the egg white and shrimp together well. Place the cornstarch in another medium bowl or on a plate. Set aside.

■ In a small skillet, heat the 2 teaspoons oil over medium heat until the surface shimmers. Add the green onions, garlic, and ginger. Stir to combine and let cook for 1 to 2 minutes to take the rawness off the aromatics. It's okay if there's a bit of browning. Turn off the heat and set aside.

■ In a 4-quart Dutch oven or a wok, add vegetable oil to a depth of about 1 inch. Heat over medium heat to 350 degrees F. Meanwhile, place one-quarter of the shrimp in the cornstarch to coat, gently shaking off any excess. Once the oil is ready, carefully place the shrimp in the oil. Fry for about 3 minutes, turning occasionally to fry evenly. The shrimp will be lightly golden. Using a slotted spoon or tongs, transfer the shrimp to a plate lined with paper towels. Repeat with the remaining shrimp. ⟶

■ Arrange the shrimp on a serving dish. Sprinkle the salt-and-pepper mixture over the shrimp. Top with the onion mixture. If there's any salt-and-pepper mix left, serve it on the side. You can serve the shrimp as an appetizer or include it as part of a meal and serve with rice.

MOM SAYS: I prefer using shrimp in the shell. But it does take more (dirty) work to devein shrimp. If you have my first book, *Chinese Soul Food*, there's a recipe for Salt and Sichuan Pepper Shrimp that uses shrimp in the shell. Salt-and-pepper crab is also fantastic. That's another level of commitment to make at home, but do try it sometime at a Chinese restaurant.

Fried rice can take on so many personalities. Its simplest expression is egg fried rice cooked *with* green onions (not raw on top). From there, the combinations are limited only by imagination or what's available in your refrigerator. The combination of ingredients in this recipe was the result of having assorted ingredients leftover from other dishes, which is to say that you can use this as inspiration for your own creation. See page 33 for how to cut and parcook proteins that you can use for fried rice.

什錦炒飯
EVERYTHING FRIED RICE

EFFORT ● ○ ○

MAKES 4 SERVINGS, FAMILY STYLE

5 cups cold cooked rice

2 tablespoons vegetable oil, divided

2 large eggs, well beaten

2 green onions, finely chopped

1 cup bite-size broccoli florets

½ cup frozen or fresh corn kernels

½ cup sliced mushrooms, such as shiitake or cremini

1 cup proteins of your choice, such as cooked chicken, diced ham, shrimp, or whatever you have available

2 tablespoons soy sauce

Kosher salt, as needed

½ teaspoon white pepper powder

■ Fluff the rice by breaking up any clumps with your fingers or a fork. Set aside.

■ Preheat a wok over medium heat until wisps of smoke rise from the surface. Add 1 tablespoon of the vegetable oil and heat until it starts to shimmer. Add the eggs and let cook for a few seconds. Then scramble them. When the eggs are soft-cooked, not hard, turn off the heat. Transfer the eggs to a small bowl and set aside. Carefully rinse the wok and dry with a towel.

■ Return the wok to the stove over medium heat. Swirl in the remaining 1 tablespoon oil. Add the green onions and stir-fry for about 10 seconds or so to release the aroma. Add the broccoli and stir-fry for about 1 minute. Add the corn and mushrooms and stir-fry for another minute. Add the protein and stir to combine. Add the rice and egg. Stir and toss all the ingredients together, staying active to prevent sticking. If needed, turn the heat to low so that you can continue to stir and toss to mix all the ingredients thoroughly. Turn the heat back to medium and swirl the soy sauce all across the rice. Stir-fry the rice, scooping and gently tossing with the wok spatula to help incorporate the soy sauce. Once everything looks well combined, take a small bite to check for seasoning. If needed, add salt to taste. Add the white pepper and give the rice a final toss. Then transfer to a serving dish.

MOM SAYS: You can get barbecue pork from the Chinese barbecue shop to add to fried rice. Chinese sausage is also a favorite in our family.

幸
福
饗
宴

西湖牛肉羹
WEST LAKE BEEF SOUP

EFFORT ●○○

MAKES 4 TO 6 SERVINGS, FAMILY STYLE

FOR THE BEEF:

4 ounces beef, such as flank steak or "stir-fry" meat, roughly minced

1 teaspoon soy sauce

½ teaspoon cornstarch

2 teaspoons vegetable oil

FOR THE SOUP:

4 cups water or chicken broth

1½ to 2 teaspoons kosher salt

2 green onions, finely chopped, divided

½ cup very finely chopped cilantro leaves and stems, divided

½ teaspoon white pepper powder

3 tablespoons cornstarch

2 large eggs, well beaten

2 teaspoons sesame oil

This is a soup that's common on Chinese restaurant menus, and we enjoy making it at home because it's so simple and it's packed with the fresh flavors of cilantro and green onions. It's named after West Lake in Hangzhou, which is southwest of Shanghai. It's typically made with egg whites, but we use the whole egg to minimize waste—or having to figure out what to do with two egg yolks.

■ To make the beef, place it in a small bowl and mix with the soy sauce. Add the cornstarch and mix well. In a wok or a small skillet, heat the oil over medium-high heat. Add the beef and break it up with a spatula. Brown the meat, stirring occasionally, for about 2 minutes. Transfer back to the small bowl. Set aside.

■ To make the soup, bring the water to boil over high heat in a 4-quart soup pot. Then reduce the heat to medium-low. Add the beef, salt to taste, and half the green onions and cilantro, and stir to combine. Stir in the white pepper. Let simmer for 2 to 3 minutes. Mix the cornstarch with 3 tablespoons water in a liquid measuring cup with a spout. Make sure it's well combined. Slowly pour the slurry into the soup while stirring. Let it come back to a simmer. Simmer for about 1 minute or so, stirring occasionally to let the starch cook through. Swirl in the beaten egg in a fine stream and stir immediately so there aren't big clumps of egg. Add the sesame oil and remaining cilantro and onion. Serve hot.

> MOM SAYS: The white pepper, cilantro, and green onions make all the difference in the flavor of this soup. I add these ingredients generously.

Fish balls most often end up in soups or hot pots. But they're great in stir-fries too. You can use any mixture of vegetables, though we like Chinese cabbage best. Fish balls tend to contain salt, so be mindful when you're seasoning. Start conservatively and adjust amounts as needed.

■ In a small bowl, combine the water, soy sauce, hoisin sauce, oyster sauce, and green onions. Set aside.

■ Preheat a wok over high heat until wisps of smoke rise from the surface. Swirl in 1 teaspoon of the vegetable oil and let heat for a few seconds until the surface starts to shimmer. Add the fish balls and spread into a single layer. Let sear for about 30 seconds, or until you get some nicely browned edges. Flip and sear for about 15 seconds or so. Then stir-fry actively to even out the cooking, about 1 minute. Turn off the heat and transfer the fish balls to a plate or work bowl and set aside.

■ Turn the heat back to high and add the remaining 1 teaspoon vegetable oil. Since the wok is already hot, there's no need to preheat. Add the cabbage and stir-fry for about 1 minute. Add the snow peas and mushrooms. Stir-fry for about 1 minute. Add the sauce mixture and stir-fry for about 1 minute. Add the sesame oil and white pepper. Give it one last stir and transfer to a serving dish. Serve with rice.

MOM SAYS: We prefer the Venus brand of fish balls (not the cuttlefish; the labels are the same and it's easy to miss the difference in words, so pay attention). But there are many brands and styles. You can get fish balls filled with roe too, though be very careful when biting into one. The filling becomes lava on your tongue.

素菜炒魚丸
STIR-FRIED FISH BALLS AND VEGETABLES

EFFORT ●○○

MAKES 4 SERVINGS, FAMILY STYLE

2 tablespoons water

1 teaspoon soy sauce

½ teaspoon hoisin sauce

½ teaspoon oyster sauce (optional)

1 green onion, finely chopped

2 teaspoons vegetable oil, divided

1 (8-ounce) pack of fish balls, such as Venus brand; cut the fish balls in half

2 cups sliced (about 2 inches wide, ½ inch thick) Chinese cabbage

8 snow peas, trimmed (optional)

¼ cup sliced (¼ inch thick) mushrooms, such as shiitake, oyster, or cremini

½ teaspoon sesame oil

⅛ teaspoon white pepper powder

Dragon Boat Festival

Fifth Day, Fifth Month

DRAGON BOAT FESTIVAL RECIPES

龍
舟
節

WHAT'S DRAGON BOAT FESTIVAL?

端午快樂!
Duān wǔ jié kuàilè!
Happy Dragon Boat Festival!

We know it's the season for the Dragon Boat Festival when the supplies for making zongzi show up in quantity at the Asian markets. Piles of dried bamboo leaves, balls of twine, glutinous rice, peanuts, red beans, and other ingredients signal the moment. Soon, zongzi makers will be steaming up their kitchens, boiling these bundles of sticky rice filled with treasures. Not that you have to make your own. Markets fill their freezers with frozen zongzi and specialty shops load up their displays with house-made varieties. Small, medium, large, triangular, tubular, sweet, or savory, zongzi have a range of profiles. Some folks call these rice dumplings or rice tamales. The word *dumpling* is inadequate, but there is only this one word in English to describe a panoply of foods involving a wrapper and fillings. A tamale is its own art. We prefer calling zongzi by their (Mandarin) name.

How did zongzi get a festival? The legend from 278 BCE during the Warring States period in ancient China describes a poet politician named Qu Yuan who was too frank with his opinions and advice. Despite his loyalty as a minister to the state of Chu, his superiors disregarded him and he ended up going into exile. He was so distraught about government corruption and how vulnerable his homeland was to invasion that he drowned himself in the Miluo River as a form of protest. Local fishermen and villagers raced to save him in their boats, but they were too late. They beat drums to scare away spirits and fish, and they threw rice into the river as an offering to Qu Yuan. This evolved into the modern-day dragon boat races and the enjoyment of zongzi. It wasn't until during the Jin dynasty (265–420), however, that zongzi became the official food associated with the Dragon Boat Festival.

Dragon Boat Festival is also known as Duān Wǔ Jié, which refers to the summer solstice, when the sun is at its optimal position. If you happen to live where there is a dragon boat community, you might get to catch some races. Dragon boats—so called because the canoe-like boats have hand-carved and painted dragon heads at the bow—are about forty feet long and accommodate eighteen to twenty people. There's also a drummer who keeps the pace and a sweep who steers and controls when the paddlers need to speed up. Unlike rowing crew, dragon boat paddlers face and propel forward with powerful up and down motions. Traditional boats often come from multigenerational makers.

The Dragon Boat Festival is also associated with warding off evil spirits and disease. People believe this time of year is dangerous to people's health due to the return of certain insects and germs. Hanging pouches filled with mugwort and calamus was thought to help prevent disease. Bathing in medicine-infused water was also thought to protect against illness.

Mostly, the festival is about dragon boat races and indulging in a lot of sticky rice.

MEILEE'S PERSPECTIVE: I LEARNED IT FROM NI HAO, KAI-LAN

Many people can sympathize with the struggle of never seeing yourself represented in the media. The female protagonists of movies are always pencil-thin white women with dirty-blond hair and blue eyes. Every girl was perfect and somehow could stay that way without struggle. There were never any Chinese dolls or books about young Chinese American girls. If you are a little Chinese girl who needs a Halloween costume, why not be Mulan? There's nothing wrong with Mulan, but when that is the only representation anywhere close to yourself in mainstream media, it gets old.

Hope appeared in the beloved children's TV show, *Ni Hao, Kai-Lan*. It was a breath of fresh air. The show featured the adventures of Kai-Lan, a Chinese American girl, and her animal friends. She was a girl like me, navigating the ups and downs of childhood. She honored her Chinese heritage while embracing the universal themes of friendship, empathy, and problem-solving. I saw myself reflected in her experiences, from celebrating Lunar New Year or the Dragon Boat Festival to learning how to share with her friends.

Through Kai-Lan, I discovered the beauty of my culture and language. The show seamlessly incorporated Mandarin Chinese, allowing me to connect with my roots in a way that was both fun and educational. But *Ni Hao, Kai-Lan* offered more than cultural enrichment; it provided a valuable lesson in diversity and inclusion. Kai-Lan's group of friends spanned various ethnicities and backgrounds, teaching me that our differences were something to be celebrated, not hidden away. It was a powerful message for a young, impressionable viewer like me.

I recently rewatched a few episodes of *Ni Hao, Kai-Lan* with a group of all-white friends. (We were bored and wanted something to do.) The first episode was about the Dragon Boat Festival. The characters in the show taught us how to do a dragon dance. My friends and I followed along, our laughter drowning out the sound of the show. Kai-Lan and her friends raced in dragon boats across the river to get to the famed Mr. Dragon, who awaited them onshore. My friends and I cheered, watching as their race began. But Kai-Lan's boat lost the race because her teammate didn't paddle in unison. He assumed that paddling faster would help them win. The lesson for Kai-Lan and her friends was the importance of working together and how not to be a sore loser.

It was awesome to see how enthusiastic my friends were about learning the new phrases, songs, and dance. After ages of worrying about how people would judge me for my identity, it made me happy to finally see how well things had evolved.

As I grew up with this new example of representation, I began to appreciate the significance of representation in the media. The impact of seeing someone who looked like me on-screen was immeasurable. It showed me that my story, my heritage, and my experiences mattered and deserved to be shared with the world.

Ni Hao, Kai-Lan gave me the confidence to embrace my identity and culture proudly. It encouraged me to create my own narratives and share them with others, knowing that there was a place for diverse voices in the world of storytelling.

幸
福
饗
宴

白粽
PLAIN ZONGZI

VEGAN
EFFORT ●●●
MAKES 8 TO 10 SMALL ZONGZI

2 cups sweet rice, such as
Sho-Chiku-Bai

20 bamboo leaves

8 to 10 strands of kitchen twine,
about 25 inches long each

This is how Lau Lau grew up eating zongzi: plain and dipped in white sugar. This basic recipe is in honor of that childhood memory. You can also try it with brown sugar or pair it with your choice of savory condiments.

■ Place the rice in a large bowl. Cover with water by 2 inches and set aside. Fill a large pot with enough water to accommodate the width of a large bamboo leaf. Stack the leaves and gently arc them all so they will fit in the pot as if you were lining the pot with leaves. Alternatively, use a large storage tub or roasting pan that can accommodate the leaves. Let the rice and the bamboo leaves soak overnight.

■ The next day, drain the rice and the bamboo leaves. Place the bamboo leaves on a rimmed baking sheet, making sure to gently shake off any dripping water. If there are any particularly large stems, trim them off so they don't poke a hole in the zongzi.

■ To fill, layer two bamboo leaves together, slightly offset, but keep the stem ends together. Fold the leaves about a third of the way up from the stem end and create a cone. Fill with 4 tablespoons of rice. Fold the long ends of the bamboo leaves over the cone, making sure to cover any gaps. Continue wrapping the leaf around the cone until the pouch is sealed. Wrap a string around the zongzi several times, making sure the leaves are secure around the rice and there aren't any gaps. Repeat with the remaining materials.

■ To cook, bring a large pot of water to boil. Add the zongzi to the pot. Add more water as needed to submerge the zongzi. Reduce heat to low and let simmer for 1 hour. Check occasionally to add water as needed. After 1 hour, turn off the heat and transfer the zongzi to a plate or baking tray to cool for a few minutes. You can eat them while they're still warm or at room temperature. Refrigerate any leftovers. To reheat in the microwave, cut the string and loosen the bamboo leaves, then heat for 1 minute, or until the inside is warm. Alternatively, steam for 7 to 10 minutes to reheat.

> **MOM SAYS:** You can freeze zongzi and boil or steam them to reheat. Make sure to seal them well in a ziplock freezer bag or, better yet, vacuum seal them.

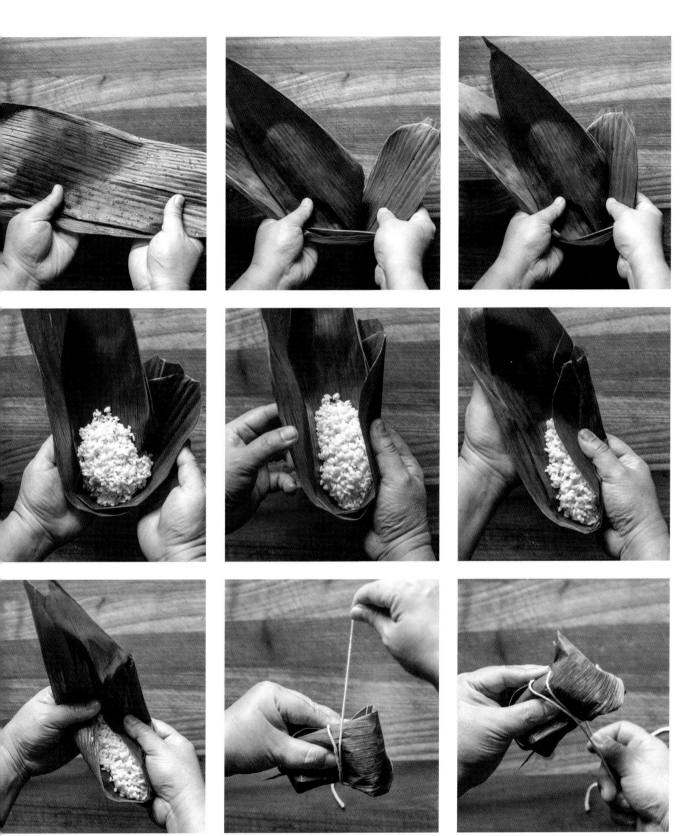

We're big fans of red bean paste in all sorts of buns and dumplings. Zongzi are no exception. Chilling or freezing the red bean paste helps to make it easier to handle. You can make your own red bean paste, but it's so much more convenient to buy it from the store. It's also known by the Japanese term "adzuki" bean paste. You will have leftover red bean paste that you can use for other purposes.

■ Place the rice in a large bowl. Cover with water by 2 inches and set aside. Fill a large pot with enough water to accommodate the width of a large bamboo leaf. Stack the leaves and gently arc them all so they will fit in the pot as if you were lining the pot with leaves. Alternatively, use a large storage tub or roasting pan that can accommodate the leaves. Let the rice and the bamboo leaves soak overnight.

■ Line a small baking dish, tray, or dinner plate with parchment paper. Scoop 1 heaping tablespoon of red bean paste and place on the parchment. Make nine more scoops of red bean paste. Cover loosely with plastic wrap and refrigerate or freeze overnight. This will make it easier to fill the zongzi.

■ The next day, drain the rice and the bamboo leaves. Place the bamboo leaves on a rimmed baking sheet, making sure to gently shake off any dripping water. If there are any particularly large stems, trim them off so they don't poke a hole in the zongzi. Get the red bean paste scoops from the refrigerator or freezer. Loosen them from the parchment as needed.

■ To fill, layer two bamboo leaves together, slightly offset, but keep the stem ends together. Fold the leaves about a third of the way up from the stem end and create a cone. Add 2 tablespoons of rice. Add a piece of red bean paste. Cover with 2 more tablespoons of rice. Fold the long ends of the bamboo leaves over the cone, making sure to cover any gaps. Continue wrapping the leaf around the cone until the pouch is sealed. Wrap a string around the zongzi several times, making sure the leaves are secure around the rice and there aren't any gaps. Repeat with the remaining materials. ⟶

紅豆粽
RED BEAN ZONGZI

VEGAN

EFFORT ●●●

MAKES 8 TO 10 SMALL ZONGZI

2 cups sweet rice, such as Sho-Chiku-Bai

20 bamboo leaves

1 package (about 10 ounces) red bean paste, chilled

8 to 10 strands of kitchen twine, about 25 inches long each

■ To cook, bring a large pot of water to boil. Add the zongzi to the pot. Add more water as needed to submerge the zongzi. Reduce heat to low and let simmer for 1 hour. Check occasionally to add water as needed. After 1 hour, turn off the heat and transfer the zongzi to a plate or baking tray to cool for a few minutes. You can eat them while they're still warm or at room temperature. Refrigerate any leftovers. To reheat in the microwave, cut the string and loosen the bamboo leaves, then heat for 1 minute, or until the inside is warm. Alternatively, steam for 7 to 10 minutes to reheat.

MOM SAYS: Technically, you could cook the plain zongzi and then spread the red bean paste on top of the rice. I like the juxtaposition of the warm rice with the cold red bean paste. It tastes great both ways.

You can include any number of vegetables in this filling. If it stir-fries, it can go in the zongzi. Of course, you can keep it simple and feature just one or two ingredients—a mix of mushrooms, for example. The idea to is to have a hint of savory veggies to complement the rice.

素餡粽
VEGETABLE ZONGZI

VEGAN

EFFORT ● ● ●

MAKES 8 TO 10 SMALL ZONGZI

2 cups sweet rice, such as Sho-Chiku-Bai

20 bamboo leaves

2 teaspoons vegetable oil

2 green onions, finely chopped

2 cups finely chopped Chinese cabbage

1 cup finely chopped baby bok choy

¼ cup grated carrot

3 medium dried shiitake mushrooms, soaked in warm water for 2 to 3 hours, stemmed, and finely diced, or 3 fresh cremini mushrooms, finely diced

1 tablespoon soy sauce

1 tablespoon hoisin sauce

1 teaspoon sesame oil

8 to 10 strands of kitchen twine, about 25 inches long each

■ Place the rice in a large bowl. Cover with water by 2 inches and set aside. Fill a large pot with enough water to accommodate the width of a large bamboo leaf. Stack the leaves and gently arc them all so they will fit in the pot as if you were lining the pot with leaves. Alternatively, use a large storage tub or roasting pan that can accommodate the leaves. Let the rice and the bamboo leaves soak overnight.

■ Cook the filling: Preheat a wok over high heat until wisps of smoke rise from the surface. Swirl the oil into the wok. Add the green onions and stir-fry for a few seconds. Add the cabbage, baby bok choy, carrots, and mushrooms. Stir-fry, making sure to combine the ingredients well, for 2 to 3 minutes. Add the soy sauce and hoisin sauce and stir-fry for 1 minute. Drizzle on the sesame oil. Stir to combine. Turn off the heat and transfer the vegetable mixture to a bowl. Let cool on the counter for 5 to 10 minutes. Cover with plastic wrap and refrigerate overnight.

■ The next day, drain the rice and the bamboo leaves. Place the bamboo leaves on a rimmed baking sheet, making sure to gently shake off any dripping water. If there are any particularly large stems, trim them off so they don't poke a hole in the zongzi.

■ To fill, layer two bamboo leaves together, slightly offset, but keep the stem ends together. Fold the leaves about a third of the way up from the stem end and create a cone. Add 2 tablespoons of rice. Add 1 tablespoon of vegetable filling. Cover with 2 more tablespoons of rice. Fold the long ends of the bamboo leaves over the cone, making sure to cover any gaps. Continue wrapping the leaf around the cone until the pouch is sealed. Wrap a string around the zongzi several times, making sure the leaves are secure around the rice and there aren't any gaps. Repeat with the remaining materials. ⟶

■ To cook, bring a large pot of water to boil. Add the zongzi to the pot. Add more water as needed to submerge the zongzi. Reduce heat to low and let simmer for 1 hour. Check occasionally to add water as needed. After 1 hour, turn off the heat and transfer the zongzi to a plate or baking tray to cool for a few minutes. You can eat them while they're still warm or at room temperature. Refrigerate any leftovers. To reheat in the microwave, cut the string and loosen the bamboo leaves, then heat for 1 minute, or until the inside is warm. Alternatively, steam for 7 to 10 minutes to reheat.

MOM SAYS: Some folks add peanuts and hard-cooked eggs. I personally don't like adding nuts, but feel free to make it your own.

Chinese sausage has a sweetness that goes well with sticky rice. We like the Venus brand of sweet Chinese sausages, but there are many types available. You could use Chinese duck sausage if your local Asian market sells it.

■ Place the rice in a large bowl. Cover with water by 2 inches and set aside. Fill a large pot with enough water to accommodate the width of a large bamboo leaf. Stack the leaves and gently arc them all so they will fit in the pot as if you were lining the pot with leaves. Alternatively, use a large storage tub or roasting pan that can accommodate the leaves. Let the rice and the bamboo leaves soak overnight.

■ Make the filling: In a small bowl, combine 2 tablespoons of the soy sauce, the hoisin sauce, and the oyster sauce. Stir well, then set aside. Place the chicken in another bowl. Add the remaining 1 tablespoon soy sauce. Mix well. Add the cornstarch and mix well again. In a small skillet, heat the oil over medium-high heat. Add the chicken and use a spatula to break up the pieces. Let sear for about 30 seconds or so, flip the pieces, and let sear for another 30 seconds. Add the mushrooms, sausage, and the sauce mixture. Stir to combine. Turn off the heat and transfer the filling to a bowl. Let cool on the counter for 5 to 10 minutes. Cover with plastic wrap and refrigerate overnight.

■ The next day, drain the rice and the bamboo leaves. Place the bamboo leaves on a rimmed baking sheet, making sure to gently shake off any dripping water. If there are any particularly large stems, trim them off so they don't poke a hole in the zongzi.

■ To fill, layer two bamboo leaves together, slightly offset, but keep the stem ends together. Fold the leaves about a third of the way up from the stem end and create a cone. Add 2 tablespoons of rice. Add a spoonful of filling, making sure to get a mix of chicken and sausage. Cover with 2 more tablespoons of rice. Fold the long ends of the bamboo leaves over the cone, making sure to cover any gaps. Continue wrapping the leaf around the cone until the pouch is sealed. Wrap a string around the zongzi several times, making sure the leaves are secure around the rice and there aren't any gaps. Repeat with the remaining materials. ⟶

雞肉臘腸粽
CHICKEN AND CHINESE SAUSAGE ZONGZI

EFFORT ● ● ●
MAKES 8 TO 10 SMALL ZONGZI

2 cups sweet rice, such as Sho-Chiku-Bai

20 bamboo leaves

3 tablespoons soy sauce, divided

2 tablespoons hoisin sauce

1 tablespoon oyster sauce

1 large or 2 small boneless, skinless chicken thighs, cut into ½-inch pieces

2 teaspoons cornstarch

2 teaspoons vegetable oil

3 medium dried shiitake mushrooms, soaked in warm water for 2 to 3 hours, cut into ½-inch dice

1 Chinese sausage, cut into ¼-inch dice

8 to 10 strands of kitchen twine, about 25 inches long each

■ To cook, bring a large pot of water to boil. Add the zongzi to the pot. Add more water as needed to submerge the zongzi. Reduce heat to low and let simmer for 1 hour. Check occasionally to add water as needed. After 1 hour, turn off the heat and transfer the zongzi to a plate or baking tray to cool for a few minutes. You can eat them while they're still warm or at room temperature. Refrigerate any leftovers. To reheat in the microwave, cut the string and loosen the bamboo leaves, then heat for 1 minute, or until the inside is warm. Alternatively, steam for 7 to 10 minutes to reheat.

> **MOM SAYS:** I default to shiitake mushrooms, but you don't have to stick with one kind. If you like a little crunch, you could always add wood ear mushrooms. You also can punch up the flavor with garlic or spice.

When we make red-braised pork for zongzi, we have to make a double portion because everyone ends up sneaking bites of the pork and, before we know it, there isn't enough for the rice. Allow time to soak the rice and bamboo leaves, and to braise the pork belly.

紅燒豬肉粽
RED-BRAISED PORK BELLY ZONGZI

EFFORT ● ● ●
MAKES 8 TO 10 SMALL ZONGZI

FOR THE PORK BELLY:

1 pound pork belly with skin on (the skin is essential; see note)

6 to 8 cups water, plus more as needed

½ cup soy sauce

¼ cup Shaoxing wine or mirin

2 tablespoons rock sugar

2 green onions, cut into 3-inch segments

3 slices fresh ginger, about ¼ inch thick and 3 inches long

1 star anise

FOR THE ZONGZI:

2 cups sweet rice, such as Sho-Chiku-Bai

20 bamboo leaves

8 to 10 strands of kitchen twine, about 25 inches long each

- To make the pork belly, cut the pork belly into roughly 1½-inch squares. Place the pork in a large Dutch oven and add 6 cups of water. Bring to a boil over high heat, then reduce the heat to low. Let simmer for 15 minutes, then skim off the scum that floats to the top. Add the soy sauce, wine, rock sugar, green onions, ginger, and star anise. Stir to distribute. Let simmer for 1 hour, then check the tenderness and the water level. If the pork isn't tender, continue simmering. Make sure the liquid just covers the meat. Check again after 15 minutes. If it feels mostly tender, raise the heat slightly to increase the level of simmer. Now the goal is to reduce the sauce until it starts to thicken. How much you reduce the liquid depends on your preference. If you want more sauce, you can quit cooking once the pork is tender. If you want the sauce to be syrupy, then reduce it until it reaches that sticky goodness. This might take 10 minutes or more, depending on how much liquid you have. When it's done to your liking, turn off the heat and let it cool for 20 minutes. Transfer the pork and sauce to a storage container and put it in the refrigerator.

- To make the zongzi, place the rice in a large bowl. Cover with water by 2 inches and set aside. Fill a large pot with enough water to accommodate the width of a large bamboo leaf. Stack the leaves and gently arc them all so they will fit in the pot as if you were lining the pot with leaves. Alternatively, use a large storage tub or roasting pan that can accommodate the leaves. Let the rice and the bamboo leaves soak overnight.

- The next day, drain the rice and the bamboo leaves. Place the bamboo leaves on a rimmed baking sheet, making sure to gently shake off any dripping water. If there are any particularly large stems, trim them off so they don't poke a hole in the zongzi. Reheat the pork and sauce, just enough so that the sauce liquefies. Slice the pork into ½-inch pieces and set aside. Strain the sauce and set aside. ⟶

■ To fill, layer two bamboo leaves together, slightly offset, but keep the stem ends together. Fold the leaves about a third of the way up from the stem end and create a cone. Add 2 tablespoons of rice. Add some pork and spoon on plenty of sauce. Top with 2 more tablespoons of rice. Fold the long ends of the bamboo leaves over the cone, making sure to cover any gaps. Continue wrapping the leaf around the cone until the pouch is sealed. Wrap a string around the zongzi several times, making sure the leaves are secure around the rice and there aren't any gaps. Repeat with the remaining materials.

■ To cook, bring a large pot of water to boil. Add the zongzi to the pot. Add more water as needed to submerge the zongzi. Reduce heat to low and let simmer for 1 hour. Check occasionally to add water as needed. After 1 hour, turn off the heat and transfer the zongzi to a plate or baking tray to cool for a few minutes. You can eat them while they're still warm or at room temperature. Refrigerate any leftovers. To reheat in the microwave, cut the string and loosen the bamboo leaves, then heat for 1 minute, or until the inside is warm. Alternatively, steam for 7 to 10 minutes to reheat.

MOM SAYS: You may have to go to an Asian market to get pork belly with skin on. The skin has collagen, which is what gives the sauce its unctuousness. This sauce is what Meilee and Shen call "yummy sauce."

ngzi from Mee Sum Cafe in New York City's Chinatown.

Mid-Autumn Festival

Fifteenth Day, Eighth Month

MID-AUTUMN FESTIVAL RECIPES

中
秋
節

WHAT'S MID-AUTUMN FESTIVAL?

中秋快樂!
Zhōng qiū kuài lè!
Happy Mid-Autumn Festival!

When gorgeous boxes of mooncakes arrive at Asian markets, you know that the Mid-Autumn Festival is around the corner. Also called the Moon Festival, it's the second most significant time of year after Lunar New Year. It's like Thanksgiving in that people go home to be with family, indulge in a big reunion feast (tuan yuan), light up the night with lanterns or send sky lanterns floating, and share mooncakes while admiring the moon. There are similar harvest celebrations that take place in countries throughout Asia, including Chuseok in Korea, Tsukimi in Japan, and Tet Trung Thu in Vietnam. Communities in Singapore, Malaysia, Indonesia, and the Philippines also celebrate the Mid-Autumn Festival. Cambodians celebrate the Water and Moon Festival later in November.

The festival takes place after the fall harvest season, so the celebration meal features seasonal foods. In China, that might include hairy crab, river snails, pumpkins, taro, lotus root, pears, pomelo, pomegranate, and duck. In Taiwan, some variations on must-have foods include sweet potatoes, pineapple cakes, and grilled foods—a contemporary tradition that began when a Taiwanese maker of soy sauce and other condiments wanted to sell more barbecue sauce and suggested people grill foods outdoors while viewing the moon. It caught on and is now a popular activity during the Mid-Autumn Festival. These foods represent family togetherness, good luck, fertility (pomegranate), and wishes for a happy life. While grilled meats don't have a particular symbolic meaning, they do bring people together and that, ultimately, is the goal.

The origin story of mooncakes involves peasants hiding messages of rebellion in mooncakes to signal an uprising against the Mongols during the Yuan dynasty (1279–1368). The message was to strike on the fifteenth day of the eighth month, and this is now the day that Mid-Autumn Festival, or Moon Festival, takes place.

The mooncakes themselves vary in style from region to region. What's universal is the round shape, which mimics the full moon and represents wholeness and family unity. Cantonese-style mooncakes with the golden crust are most commonly recognized. Even the mooncake emoji is Cantonese. Fillings include a combination of ingredients, such as nuts, red bean paste, lotus, mung bean, and salted egg yolk. Other styles of mooncakes may have a flaky white pastry or a short crust. Some styles include meat or black sesame paste. Contemporary interpretations include the "snowy" mooncakes, which are mochi-like and translucent. Newer generations of Asian cooks have been experimenting with fillings that contain durian, fig, red dates, mango, passion fruit, custard, molten chocolate, tea or coffee flavors, and even pecan pie. Once someone broke down the walls of tradition, creativity could flow freely into these sweets.

We sometimes joke that traditional mooncakes are like fruitcakes. They're so rich and dense that you can barely eat a fraction of one. (We may have regifted a box or two in our lifetime, ahem.) But with these modern takes on mooncake flavors, we may have to retire that joke.

Speaking of gifts, every year, it seems like the packaging for mooncake boxes gets sleeker and fancier, with prices that match. During a recent trip to an Asian market in Seattle, boxes of mooncakes cost anywhere from $25 to nearly $100. That's astounding. We've also noticed non-Asian companies trying to capitalize on the Mid-Autumn Festival (as well as Lunar New Year) with themed treats. MarieBelle chocolates, for example, offers a deluxe mooncake set.

Mid-Autumn Festival is thought to have originated during the Shang dynasty (1600 to 1050 BCE) to honor the moon goddess for the bountiful harvest. The first recorded mention of the festival, however, didn't appear until the subsequent Zhou dynasty. The legend is that Chang'e became the moon goddess after drinking the immortality elixir that had been intended for her husband, Hou Yi. Hou Yi was a famous archer who shot down nine of ten suns to prevent the earth from being scorched. The gods gave Hou Yi this elixir, but there was only enough for one and he didn't want immortality without his wife at his side. But Chang'e drank it and floated to the moon to live forever. There are a few different versions of this myth with differing details about how Chang'e came to find this elixir and whether she was trying to protect it from a thief or if she wanted to escape from her husband. One version also mentions Chang'e having a rabbit companion, which is why there are rabbit lanterns during the Mid-Autumn Festival. Either way, Chang'e ended up living on the moon and Hou Yi would leave out her favorite foods under the moonlight.

The Feast

Having mooncakes to eat and share is essential. While the menu features a few seasonal foods that symbolize family togetherness and good luck, you certainly can make the feast with whatever dishes you choose. What would make you happy to eat? What would your guests enjoy eating? Feel free to borrow recipes you like from other chapters to serve at this celebration. Sharing a meal of your choice with your people of choice is what matters—and finishing the night with some mooncakes.

A sample menu from this chapter plus a couple of items from other chapters:

- Egg Drop Soup with Dungeness Crab
- Sweet Potato Fritters
- Clams with Aromatics and Chinese Black Beans
- Chicken with Carrots and Mushrooms
- Super-Garlicky Baby Bok Choy (page 181)
- Garlic Shrimp with Gai Lan (page 69)
- Barbecue Duck (from the Chinese barbecue shop)
- Mooncakes (store-bought or homemade)

Feel free to mix it up!

MEILEE'S PERSPECTIVE: DOES ANYONE EVEN LIKE MOONCAKES?

Mooncakes, those peculiar little pastries that grace our homes every year during the Mid-Autumn Festival, are the subject of much debate: Does anyone even like mooncakes?

The Mid-Autumn Festival, also known as the Moon Festival, honors unity, coming together with your family and loved ones, and the harvest. Mooncakes are an integral part of this celebration, and they come in an array of flavors and fillings. From lotus seed paste to red bean paste and black sesame to durian, there's a mooncake for every palate. But here's the thing—do we really love them, or are we eating them only to please our ancestors?

As a picky eater, I have built up the courage to take only a nibble out of a mooncake. I like red bean paste as a filling, but the idea of what a mooncake would taste like has often scared me. I prefer to stick with a classic scallion pancake or baked red bean bun.

Across social media, mooncakes are often the subject of jokes and memes. People frequently compare mooncakes to doorstops, hockey pucks, or worse. Yet, as with many traditions, mooncakes have their staunch supporters. You'll find many people who savor the traditional flavors passed down through generations.

Many people, year after year, go through the motions of buying, gifting, and eating mooncakes, all while secretly wondering if they're the only ones not head over heels for these dense pastries. The truth is, it's perfectly fine not to like mooncakes, and it's time we accept that.

Traditions can and should evolve. While traditional mooncakes hold a special place in the hearts of many, they aren't everyone's cup of tea. This doesn't mean we should abandon the Mid-Autumn Festival or disrespect its cultural significance. Instead, it's an opportunity to adapt and evolve traditions.

Lately mooncakes have been getting a modern twist. People have been experimenting with new flavors and textures, hoping to entice a wider audience. We've seen mooncakes filled with chocolate, mochi, and even ice cream. These contemporary renditions are a nod to the fact that traditions can be flexible and cater to diverse tastes.

If you love them, great! If not, that's perfectly fine too. So the next time someone offers you a mooncake, know that just because you have to receive it with gratitude doesn't mean you have to like it. And you can laugh inside at the idea of these edible doorstops. The important thing is to cherish that togetherness that the Mid-Autumn Festival represents.

Mooncake selection at Po Wing Hong Market in New York.

This style of mooncake has a flaky crust and is unlike the more commonly recognized Cantonese-style mooncakes. You can fill it with sweet or savory ingredients. Red bean paste is our go-to flavor—without inclusions, such as egg yolk. We like to keep it straightforward. You will have leftover red bean paste that you can use for other purposes. To add a design to the top of the mooncakes, you'll need a cotton swab or rounded makeup applicator swab or a food-safe fine-tipped paintbrush.

酥皮紅豆月餅
FLAKY RED BEAN MOONCAKES

EFFORT ● ● ●

MAKES 16 TO 18 MOONCAKES

2 cups all-purpose flour, divided, plus more for dusting

8 tablespoons very cold unsalted butter, cut into ½-inch dice

6 tablespoons cold water, divided

8 tablespoons cold vegetable shortening

1 package (about 10 ounces) red bean paste, chilled

1 to 2 drops red food dye, mixed with a drop of water (optional)

■ In a medium bowl, combine 1 cup of the flour with the butter. Using a pastry cutter or your hands, work the butter into the flour, making sure the butter gets evenly distributed. If you're using your hands, you can rub the flour-coated pieces of butter between your fingers to mash them a bit. But don't go overboard, because you want the butter to stay cold. Stir in 3 tablespoons of the water, then gather the mixture together to form a ball. Knead it a few times to smooth it out. Set aside.

■ In another bowl, combine the remaining 1 cup flour with the vegetable shortening. Similar to the butter dough, use a pastry cutter or your hands to work the shortening into the flour until there are no large chunks of shortening left. Stir in the remaining 3 tablespoons water, then gather the mixture together to form a ball. Knead a few times to smooth it out. Roll this dough into a rope that's about 12 inches long. Set aside.

■ Dust your work surface with flour. Roll out the butter dough until you have a rectangle that's about 12 by 6 inches. Place the rope of shortening dough across the middle of the rectangle, and wrap the butter dough around the shortening dough. Seal the seam and smooth it out by rolling the tube of dough a few times until you get a rope that's about 20 inches long. Cut the dough into sixteen pieces. Roll each piece into a ball. Place on a small baking sheet lined with parchment paper. Cover loosely with plastic wrap and place in the refrigerator to chill for at least 30 minutes.

■ Preheat the oven to 375 degrees F. ⟶

■ Press a piece of dough with your fingers or use a small rolling pin to roll out the dough to about 2¼ inches in diameter. Add about 1 teaspoon of red bean paste. If you get any on your fingers, be sure to wipe them clean before the next step. Gather the dough around the filling and seal the seam. It won't look pretty, but that's okay. Roll between your palms to smooth out the seam. Press gently between your palms to create a puck-like shape. Set on a baking sheet lined with parchment paper. Press down gently to flatten the puck as needed. Repeat with the remaining dough.

■ If you want to decorate the mooncakes, dip a cotton swab in the red dye mixture and dab a design on the tops of the mooncakes. It could be as simple as a few dots or a smiley face or something more elaborate. Usually, the designs on the mooncakes are decorative or they denote the filling.

■ Bake the mooncakes for 30 minutes, or until the bottom of the pastry is lightly browned. Let cool for a few minutes before trying to eat one. The filling will be very hot.

MOM SAYS: I taught myself how to make this style of mooncake when I was a teenager. We had several Wei-Chuan cookbooks and I had to learn how to decipher translated instructions. At the time, I fantasized about opening a pastry shop. While I abandoned that idea long ago, I still love to bake.

Family meals in our house often include a chicken dish because it's Meilee's favorite protein. Late-summer and fall mushrooms, such as morels, chanterelles, matsutake, lobster, and others, would work in this dish and fit the Mid-Autumn Festival harvest theme. Highlight one type of mushroom or use a mix.

蘑菇雞絲 + 胡蘿蔔絲
CHICKEN
with Carrots and Mushrooms

EFFORT ●○○

MAKES 4 SERVINGS, FAMILY STYLE

8 ounces chicken breast

2 tablespoons soy sauce, divided

2 teaspoons cornstarch

2 tablespoons vegetable oil, divided

1½ cups seasonal mushrooms, such as chanterelles, or your favorite mushrooms

½ cup sliced (¼ inch thick) carrots

2 large cloves garlic, crushed

2 tablespoons water

¼ teaspoon sesame oil

■ Cut the chicken breast lengthwise into two to three strips, about 1½ inches wide, or about the size of chicken tenders. Then slice each strip of chicken crosswise into slivers. The exact size of the slivers is not as important as keeping the pieces relatively uniform. In a small bowl, combine the chicken with 1 tablespoon of the soy sauce and mix well. Add the cornstarch and mix well again.

■ Preheat a wok over high heat until wisps of smoke rise from the surface. Add 1 tablespoon of the vegetable oil and heat until it shimmers. Add the chicken and, using a spatula, quickly spread it into a single layer in the bowl of the wok. After about 15 seconds, stir-fry the chicken for about 1 more minute, or until the chicken is nearly cooked through. Remove the wok from the heat, transfer the chicken to a small bowl, and set aside. Rinse the wok and dry with a towel.

■ Return the wok to the stove over high heat. Swirl in the remaining 1 tablespoon vegetable oil and heat until it starts to shimmer. Add the mushrooms and carrots and spread out in the wok. Let sear for about 10 seconds or so, then stir and let sear a few more seconds. Add the chicken and stir-fry for about 1 minute. Add the remaining 1 tablespoon soy sauce, garlic, and water. Stir-fry for 1 to 2 minutes more, or until the mushrooms have softened. Drizzle with the sesame oil and transfer to a serving dish.

MOM SAYS: You can get wild foraged mushrooms at your local farmers' market. They can be more expensive than the cultivated mushrooms you find at the supermarket. Use the mushrooms that you prefer and have access to.

辣味亞洲梨柚子沙拉

ASIAN PEAR AND POMELO SALAD
with Chili Crisp Vinaigrette

VEGETARIAN

EFFORT ●○○

MAKES 4 SERVINGS, FAMILY STYLE

2 small stalks celery heart with the leaves (the light-green inner stalks), sliced ¼ inch thick on the bias, including the leaves

1 medium carrot, peeled and cut into very fine 3-inch strips

1 pomelo, segmented and membrane removed

1 medium Asian pear (preferably 20th Century), cored and sliced into fine strips

2 tablespoons extra-virgin olive oil

1½ tablespoons soy sauce

½ tablespoon balsamic vinegar

1 teaspoon honey

1 to 2 teaspoons Fly By Jing chili crisp, or your favorite brand

The Asian pear adds a light, floral sweetness to this salad. It will hold in the refrigerator for at least a day. The pears will release their juices as they sit longer in the dressing, so do be mindful.

■ Combine the celery, carrots, pomelo, and Asian pear in a large bowl. In a small bowl, combine the olive oil, soy sauce, balsamic vinegar, and honey. Whisk together well. Stir in the chili crisp to taste.

■ Drizzle the dressing over the salad and toss well to combine. Serve as an accompaniment or as a starter.

MOM SAYS: Search online for a video on how to supreme citrus fruits. This is where you shave off the rind of the citrus and make angled cuts along the membranes to release the pulp. When you want to incorporate citrus into salads, this makes all the difference for the eating experience.

We love getting a whole roasted duck from the Chinese barbecue shop, but we usually have leftover duck. Perhaps we intentionally leave some duck so that we can make duck soup the next day. Whether you use leftover duck or you buy a quarter or half a duck specifically for soup, the method is straightforward and it doesn't take a whole lot of time to make.

■ In a medium soup pot, combine the duck and water. Bring to a boil over high heat, then turn the heat to low. Let simmer for about 5 minutes. Skim any scum off the surface. Add the green onions, ginger, cabbage, preserved mustard greens, and white pepper. Stir to combine. Let simmer for 20 minutes.

■ Taste the broth. The preserved mustard greens are very salty and that's what helps to season the soup. If it doesn't taste salty enough, you can either add ¼ cup more of the mustard greens or salt to taste. Add the bean thread and let simmer for 5 minutes, or until the noodles have rehydrated and are clear. If the water level seems low, add a cup of water and stir. Top with chopped cilantro and serve.

MOM SAYS: If you like spicy foods, you can get spicy preserved mustard greens. For example, the Chongqing Fishwell brand of preserved mustard leaf comes in a 70-gram package and really packs a punch with savory spice. You could use one packet in your soup, if you'd like.

酸菜烤鴨濃湯
BARBECUE DUCK SOUP
with Pickled Mustard Greens

EFFORT ●○○

MAKES 4 TO 6 SERVINGS, FAMILY STYLE

¼ to ½ whole barbecue duck (or leftovers)

5 cups water, or enough to cover the duck

2 green onions, cut into 2-inch segments

3 slices ginger, about ¼ inch thick and 2 inches long

1 cup sliced Chinese cabbage (optional)

½ cup diced preserved Chinese mustard greens, plus more as needed

¼ teaspoon white pepper powder

1 bundle bean thread

½ cup finely chopped fresh cilantro (optional)

幸
福
饗
宴

辣味牛肉片炒豆乾
BEEF
with Pickled Jalapeños and Spiced Tofu

EFFORT ●○○

MAKES 4 SERVINGS, FAMILY STYLE

8 ounces flank steak

2 tablespoons soy sauce, divided

2 teaspoons cornstarch

1 tablespoon water

2 cloves garlic, minced

2 tablespoons hoisin sauce

1½ tablespoons vegetable oil, divided

8 ounces spiced tofu (see page 22), sliced ⅛ inch thick

1 to 2 tablespoons sliced pickled jalapeño

In late summer to early fall, you might come across folks who sell freshly roasted chili peppers at the farmers' market or a great grocery store. We enjoy mixing it up by incorporating freshly roasted chilies in this dish. For this recipe, we've included pickled jalapeño slices because the acidity and spice add zing and because they're widely available.

■ Trim the flank steak of any large pieces of membrane. Cut the flank in half or thirds lengthwise, or with the grain. Depending on the total width of the flank, you may get two or three sections that are about 3 inches wide. Cut these sections against the grain into ⅛-inch slices. Place the beef in a medium bowl. Add 1 tablespoon soy sauce and mix well. Then add the cornstarch and mix well again. Set aside.

■ In a small dish, combine the remaining 1 tablespoon soy sauce, water, garlic, and hoisin sauce. Stir to combine. Set aside.

■ Preheat a wok over high heat until wisps of smoke rise from the surface. Swirl in 1 tablespoon of the vegetable oil and heat until it starts to shimmer. Gently add the beef and, using a wok spatula, spread it into a single layer. Sear for about 30 seconds and then stir-fry for 1 to 2 minutes, or until the meat has browned. It's okay if there are some pieces that are undercooked. Turn off the heat and transfer the beef back to the same bowl. Set aside.

■ Scrape off any bits and pieces on the surface of the wok. If needed, give it a light scrub and rinse in the sink, being mindful that the wok is still very hot. Return the wok to high heat. Swirl in the remaining ½ tablespoon vegetable oil. Let heat for about 10 seconds. Add the tofu and spread into a single layer. Let sear for about 30 seconds and then stir. Add the jalapeño slices and beef. Stir-fry for about 1 minute. Swirl in the sauce mixture and stir-fry for 1 more minute. Turn off the heat and transfer to a serving dish.

MOM SAYS: We love Rio Luna nacho sliced jalapeños in our stir-fries. You can use the brand you prefer or try different ones!

Since sweet potatoes are available throughout the year, we don't necessarily associate them with fall. But it's included among the foods that one might enjoy for the Mid-Autumn Festival. Since Lau Lau loves sweet potatoes and we try to include everyone's favorites, we thought these fritters should be a part of our celebration. The pungent combination of Chinese chives with sweet potatoes works well.

■ Steam the bag of sweet potatoes in the microwave per the instructions on the bag. The sweet potatoes need to be cooked through enough to mash. Transfer to a medium bowl and, using a fork or a masher, mash the sweet potatoes until mostly smooth. It's okay if there are some tiny bits remaining. Scrape the mashed potatoes into the bowl of a stand mixer. Add the sweet rice flour. Mix on medium-low until the potatoes and flour are well combined. Add ¾ teaspoon of the kosher salt and the Chinese chives. Mix on low until all the ingredients are combined. Set aside. If you don't have a stand mixer, you can mix by hand in a large bowl. The sweet potatoes will be hot, so use a stiff spatula or a wooden spoon.

■ In a 4-quart Dutch oven or similar deep-sided pot, add enough oil so it's 2 inches deep. Heat over medium heat until the temperature reaches 350 degrees F. In the meantime, line a small baking sheet with parchment paper. Using two spoons to maneuver, scoop a heaping tablespoon of the sweet potato mixture and place on the parchment-lined baking sheet. Repeat until you've run out of mixture. ⟶

炸蕃薯團
SWEET POTATO FRITTERS

VEGAN
EFFORT ●●○
MAKES ABOUT 16 FRITTERS

1 (12-ounce) bag frozen sweet potatoes (microwaveable type)

1 cup sweet (glutinous) rice flour

1½ teaspoons kosher salt, divided

¾ cup finely chopped Chinese chives

Vegetable oil, for frying

■ Line a plate with a couple of layers of paper towel. Set aside. Once the oil reaches temperature, carefully slide several fritters into the oil. Don't overcrowd the pot. Let fry for about 2 minutes, or until the edges start to get golden. Transfer the fritters to the plate lined with the paper towels. Repeat with the remaining sweet potato batter.

■ Sprinkle the remaining ¾ teaspoon kosher salt on top of the fritters. Serve while warm.

MOM SAYS: If you don't have access to Chinese chives, you can use green onions or chives. You also can skip the onions and make these fritters sweet by sprinkling confectioners' sugar on them after they come out of the fryer. If your supermarket doesn't sell frozen sweet potatoes, you can cook and mash a pound of fresh sweet potatoes.

Clams are relatively affordable and are so simple to cook. Yet it feels luxurious to have a platter of clams show up at the table. Manila clams should be widely available, but feel free to use a different variety of clam. Freshness is more important than the specific variety.

■ Preheat a wok over high heat until wisps of smoke rise from the surface. Add the vegetable oil, immediately followed by the garlic, ginger, and green onions. Stir-fry for 15 to 20 seconds. Add the white wine and black bean sauce. Stir to combine. Add the clams and stir. Reduce the heat to medium. Cover with a lid and let steam for 7 to 8 minutes, or until the clams open. If you have a couple of clams that don't open after the steaming period, discard them. Transfer to a large bowl or deep platter and serve right away.

MOM SAYS: Be sure to buy and cook the clams the same day. If you do have to store them overnight, keep them in a bowl or on a tray and covered with a damp towel. Keep them in the coldest part of the refrigerator and use them as soon as possible. Do not submerge them in water, which will kill them.

豆豉蛤蜊
CLAMS
with Aromatics and Chinese Black Beans

EFFORT ●○○

MAKES 4 SERVINGS, FAMILY STYLE

1 teaspoon vegetable oil

3 large cloves garlic, finely chopped

½ cup finely julienned fresh ginger

2 green onions, finely chopped

¼ cup dry white wine, such as sauvignon blanc, pinot grigio, or similar

2 teaspoons black bean sauce, such as Lee Kum Kee

1½ pounds Manila clams, cleaned

幸
福
饗
宴

鄧金斯螃蟹
SAVORY DUNGENESS CRAB

EFFORT ● ● ●

MAKES 4 SERVINGS, FAMILY STYLE

2 whole live Dungeness crabs, about 4 pounds (have the fishmonger remove the carapace and clean the crab for you; you should have four halves, and each half should have four legs plus a claw)

2 teaspoons vegetable oil

6 large cloves garlic, lightly smashed and peeled

3 green onions, cut into 2-inch segments

¼ cup thinly sliced fresh ginger

¼ cup Shaoxing wine or everyday dry red wine

¼ cup soy sauce

¼ cup water

In China, they celebrate the fall harvest by eating the seasonal hairy crab, a type of burrowing crab that lives in rivers. We can't get hairy crab, but Dungeness crab is a favorite in the Pacific Northwest, where we live. When crabbing season opens, we visit family members who live on Camano Island, about sixty-five miles north of Seattle, and we go crabbing. It really doesn't get fresher than that. Meilee has become our resident crab processor, delivering a swift end for the catch. We eat some of the crabs simply boiled and dipped in butter. We also like to stir-fry some with aromatics, soy sauce, and wine. You can use the type of crab that's available to you.

■ Bring a large pot of water to boil over high heat. You'll need enough water to submerge the crab parts. Add the crab to the boiling water. Reduce the heat to medium-high to maintain an active simmer, but it doesn't need to be a rolling boil. Let cook for 12 to 15 minutes. Remove the crab from the pot and let it cool for about 5 minutes. Wear rubber gloves or an oven mitt to hold the crab legs and, with the other hand, use a crab cracker to make some cracks in each leg. Alternatively, use a meat mallet, hammer, or the dull side of a cleaver to crack the shell. This will help the sauce seep into the shell. Set aside.

■ Preheat a wok over high heat until wisps of smoke rise from the surface. Add the oil and heat until the surface shimmers. Add the garlic, green onions, and ginger. Stir-fry for a few seconds. Add the wine, soy sauce, and water. Stir to combine. Let the sauce come to a simmer and reduce the heat to medium or medium-low. You want the sauce to have some light simmering, but you don't want it to reduce too quickly. Add the crab and carefully maneuver the crab legs so that each set gets into the sauce. Let simmer for 5 to 6 minutes, occasionally stirring the crab so that each piece gets to sit in the sauce. Arrange on a platter and serve with plenty of napkins!

MOM SAYS: You can buy cold cracked Dungeness crab at most seafood counters where it's available. While you could buy pre-cooked crab and refresh it in boiling water before adding to the sauce, you risk overcooking the crab. Also, it's hard to tell how long the cooked crab has been on display. It's worth the extra attention to get the freshest crab you can.

If you want to celebrate fall harvest with crab but you don't want to go all out to have whole crab, this soup is the answer. You can use lump crab from the seafood market, and the soup is simple to put together. The ingredients are also adaptable to what's in season. In the summer, for example, we like to make corn and crab soup. For the Mid-Autumn Festival, we take advantage of the last of the summer tomatoes.

■ Preheat a 2-quart soup pot over high heat for about 15 seconds. Add the oil and heat until the oil starts to shimmer. Add the tomatoes and let cook for about 1 minute, stirring occasionally. Add the green onions, soy sauce, and ginger. Stir to combine. Add the water and corn. Stir to combine. Let the water come to a boil. Reduce the heat to medium-low.

■ Break up any large pieces of crab. You want them to be relatively bite-size without shredding them. Add the crab to the soup. Let simmer for about 5 minutes. Taste the broth. If needed, add salt to taste. Drizzle the beaten egg over the soup and stir immediately to break up any egg that has clumped together. Add the sesame oil, white pepper, and cilantro. Stir to combine. Serve in bowls, making sure that each bowl gets pieces of crab.

MOM SAYS: If you want the soup to have a bit more body, you can add a cornstarch slurry to thicken it. Mix 2 tablespoons cornstarch with 2 tablespoons water. Before adding the egg, stir in the cornstarch gently, making sure it gets distributed evenly but without destroying the chunks of crab. Then add the egg and other seasonings.

蟹肉蛋花湯
EGG DROP SOUP
with Dungeness Crab

EFFORT ● ○ ○

MAKES 4 SERVINGS, FAMILY STYLE

2 tablespoons vegetable oil

1 cup diced fresh tomatoes

2 green onions, chopped

¼ cup soy sauce

2 teaspoons grated fresh ginger

5 cups water

½ cup fresh or frozen corn kernels

1½ cups lump Dungeness crab, or crab meat of your choice

Kosher salt

2 large eggs, well beaten

½ teaspoon sesame oil

⅛ teaspoon white pepper powder (optional)

Chopped fresh cilantro, for garnish (optional)

Winter Solstice

Falls on December 21, 22, or 23

WINTER SOLSTICE RECIPES

WHAT'S DŌNGZHI?

冬至快樂!
Dōngzhi kuài lè!
Happy winter solstice!

Dōngzhi, or winter solstice, falls on December 21, 22, or 23, and marks the change from the harvest season to winter. As the shortest day of the year in the Northern Hemisphere, it also commemorates the transition toward longer days and the spring. It wasn't until the Han dynasty (206 BCE to 220 CE) when the rulers adopted the lunisolar calendar and formalized the celebration of Lunar New Year (which takes place sometime between mid-January to mid-February) that Dōngzhi became a distinct holiday.

The solstice is another occasion for families to gather to pay respects to ancestors, the gods, and to eat. Ancient traditions include honoring teachers for their expertise and giving shoes to the elderly to wish them longevity.

There are regional differences for what people eat, but tang yuan is most commonly associated with Dōngzhi. The sound of the characters for tang yuan—the same glutinous rice balls served during the Lantern Festival (see page 80)—resembles "tuan yuan," which means coming together around the table. In northern regions, jiaozi made with wheat flour (such as Pork and Cabbage Dumplings, page 57) is typical. Some people also eat wonton soup or glutinous rice cakes shaped like animals. To beat the winter cold and boost their body constitution, people infuse warming ingredients into celebration dishes. Lamb and other meats, ginger, leeks, garlic, glutinous rice, and bone broth are among the many types of warming foods.

Some say that Dōngzhi is as big a deal as Lunar New Year. We haven't experienced that, but the sentiments around both holidays are similar: it's about family near and far coming together to honor those who came before us and sharing symbolic and delicious foods.

冬至湯圓
SOLSTICE TANG YUAN

EFFORT ●●○
MAKES 24 TANG YUAN

FOR THE TANG YUAN:

1 cup glutinous rice flour, such as Mochiko Sweet Rice Flour

½ teaspoon kosher salt

Scant ½ cup warm water (about 110 degrees F)

1 drop red food dye

FOR THE SOUP:

1 teaspoon vegetable oil

2 green onions, finely chopped

1 teaspoon grated fresh ginger

2 cups sliced baby bok choy or other similar greens

2 teaspoons soy sauce

5 cups Chinese-Style Chicken Broth (page 226) or water

1 teaspoon kosher salt, plus more to taste

⅛ teaspoon white pepper powder

2 tablespoons fried shallots

½ teaspoon sesame oil

¼ cup chopped fresh cilantro

For the solstice, you can make pink tang yuan to symbolize good luck. We do half-and-half. And, instead of a sweet syrup, we serve tang yuan in a savory soup with greens. If you prefer a sweet version, try one of the recipes in the Lantern Festival chapter (page 80).

■ To make the tang yuan, in a medium bowl, combine the sweet rice flour with the salt and water. Stir together until bits of dough start to form. Then use your hand to gather the shards together into a ball of dough. Keep kneading the dough for a few minutes until it's smooth and holds together. Divide the dough in half. Cover one piece of dough loosely with plastic wrap to keep it from drying out.

■ Line a dinner plate or small tray with parchment paper and set aside. Place the remaining half of dough in a metal or glass stain-proof bowl. Press a small divot in the center of the dough and add in a drop of red dye. Wearing a food-safe rubber glove, or clean plastic bag, knead the dough until the dye is evenly distributed. Roll the pink dough into a rope about 12 inches long. Cut the dough into 8 pieces and roll each piece into a ball. Place on the parchment-lined plate. Set aside.

■ Roll the white dough into a rope about 12 inches long. Cut into 16 pieces and roll each piece into a ball. Place on the parchment-lined plate. Cover the plate loosely with plastic wrap and set aside.

■ To make the soup, in a medium pot, heat the vegetable oil over medium-high heat for about 30 seconds. Add the green onions and stir for 15 seconds. Add the ginger, bok choy, and soy sauce. Stir for 10 seconds. Add the broth or water, salt, white pepper, and fried shallots. Bring to a boil and immediately reduce heat to medium-low. Add the pink dough balls and stir to prevent sticking. Let simmer for 2 minutes, stirring occasionally. Add the white dough balls and let simmer for 5 minutes, stirring occasionally. The tang yuan will start to float when they're close to being done. Add the sesame oil and cilantro, and stir to combine. Let simmer for 2 more minutes. Serve in small bowls, making sure each person gets at least one pink tang yuan in their bowl.

MOM SAYS: Asian markets sell unfilled frozen tang yuan, which works well for this preparation. It's not imperative to make your own. The caveat is that the frozen tang yuan may not be as fresh as you'd want it. If the package has a clear window, be sure to check for freezer burn. Heavy layers of ice crystals aren't a good sign.

幸
福
饗
宴

羊肉蒜苗餃
LAMB AND LEEK DUMPLINGS

EFFORT ● ● ●
MAKES ABOUT 48 DUMPLINGS

FOR THE DOUGH:

2½ cups unbleached all-purpose flour, plus more for dusting

¾ cup warm tap water

FOR THE FILLING:

1 pound ground lamb

1 cup chopped leeks

½ teaspoon ground cumin

1 teaspoon minced fresh ginger

3 tablespoons soy sauce

¼ teaspoon white pepper powder

1 teaspoon sesame oil

Dumpling Dipping Sauce (page 58)

Lamb, leeks, and ginger are considered to have warming properties. This combination suits the spirit of the winter solstice celebration. This type of dumpling—jiaozi—comes from northern China but is a beloved food across the world.

■ To make the dough, place the flour in a large mixing bowl. Add the water and, using a rubber spatula or wooden spoon, stir the water and flour together. Continue to stir gently until a ball of dough starts to form. Start kneading the dough to make a ball. The dough should feel slightly tacky but not damp. Cover the dough with a damp towel or plastic wrap and let it rest for a minimum of 20 minutes.

■ To make the filling, combine the ground lamb, leeks, cumin, ginger, soy sauce, white pepper, and sesame oil in a medium bowl and mix well. Set aside.

■ To make the wrappers, divide the dough in half. Roll each half into a rope that's about ¾ inch in diameter and about 18 inches or so in length. Cut each rope into pieces that are about ¾ inch thick (or 9 to 10 grams). Dust your work surface and the dough pieces with flour. Roll each piece into a ball, then press it between your palms into a silver-dollar-size disk. With a 10- or 12-inch Chinese dowel-style rolling pin (available in Asian markets or online), roll each disk into a flat circle about 3 inches in diameter. Dust with flour as needed to prevent sticking. Don't worry about making a perfect circle.

■ Place a dollop of filling, about a teaspoon or so, into the center of a wrapper. Fold the round wrapper in half over the center into a half-moon shape and pinch shut along the edges. (For a tutorial on pleating, search YouTube for "Hsiao-Ching Chou and dumplings.") The dough should be just sticky enough to seal without using water or egg. Repeat until you have used up all the dough or you run out of filling.

■ To cook, fill a large soup pot with 4 quarts of water and bring to a boil over high heat. Set a 1-cup measuring cup filled with cold water next to the stove, within easy reach. When the water starts to boil, carefully add about half the prepared dumplings, or only as many as your pot can accommodate without overcrowding. Return to a boil and cook for about 5 minutes. You may have to fish out a dumpling and cut it open to confirm. Keep a close watch on the water as it will likely bubble over. Add a quick splash of the cold water to help calm down the boil and adjust the heat as needed. You want a steady boil that doesn't boil over the top of the pot. The dumplings are done when they puff up, float, and the skins are slightly translucent. Use a large slotted spoon or a spider strainer to transfer the cooked dumplings to a platter. Serve with Dumpling Dipping Sauce.

MOM SAYS: To save time, you can use store-bought dumpling wrappers. If you can get to an Asian market, look for the thicker wrappers, which may be labeled as "sui gow" (boiled dumplings). You will need to dab the edges with water to seal the dumplings.

幸
福
饗
宴

薑汁雞肉餛飩湯
GINGERY CHICKEN WONTON SOUP

EFFORT ●●○
MAKES 4 TO 6 SERVINGS

FOR THE BROTH:

6 cups Chinese-Style Chicken Broth (page 226)

1 teaspoon grated fresh ginger

FOR THE WONTONS:

1 pound ground chicken

2 green onions, finely chopped

1 tablespoon soy sauce

1 teaspoon grated fresh ginger

½ teaspoon sesame oil

⅛ teaspoon white pepper powder

1 package wonton wrappers

8 cups water

2 cups sliced baby bok choy or Chinese cabbage

Chopped fresh cilantro for garnish, optional

Wonton soup is good anytime you need a soothing bowl of comfort. For the winter solstice, we add extra ginger for warmth and spice. You could use the pork and shrimp filling from the Pork and Shrimp Fried Wontons recipe (page 191) if you prefer. Allow time to make the broth.

■ Combine the broth and ginger in a medium soup pot. Bring to a simmer over medium-high heat, then reduce heat to low. Let the ginger infuse the broth for about 15 minutes. Turn off the heat. Set aside.

■ To make the wontons, combine the ground chicken, green onions, soy sauce, ginger, sesame oil, and white pepper in a medium bowl. Mix well.

■ Line a baking sheet with parchment paper. Place ¼ cup water in a small bowl. Place a flat teaspoon's amount of filling at the center of a wonton wrapper. Dip your finger in the water and drag it along one edge of the wonton wrapper and repeat with all four sides. Fold the wrapper in half over the filling, lining up the edges and pressing down to seal. You will have a rectangular packet. Hold the rectangle with the fold side down. Now dip your finger in the water again and dab it on the underside of the right corner of the rectangle. Maneuver the wonton and bend it so that the right corner, the one you've just dabbed with water, overlaps with the left corner. Press together to seal. Place on the parchment-lined tray. Repeat with the remaining filling and wonton wrappers, then line them up in columns to optimize the space on the tray.

■ In a large pot over high heat, bring the 8 cups water to a boil. Meanwhile, add the baby bok choy to the broth and bring it back to a simmer over medium heat. Let simmer for about 5 minutes or until the bok choy is tender.

■ When the water boils, add the wontons—in batches, if needed. Stir to keep the wontons from sticking to the bottom or to each other. Cook for 2 to 3 minutes, or until the wrappers lose their opaqueness and start to glisten. Using a slotted spoon, transfer the wontons to bowls and add broth with bok choy to cover. Top with chopped cilantro and serve hot.

■ If there are leftover wontons, strain and put them in a large bowl of cold water to chill them and prevent them from sticking. Once cooled, the wontons can be strained and stored in a plastic container for several days.

MOM SAYS: With any leftover wontons, you can eat them with chili crisp and soy sauce for a quick snack. I usually add a splash of soy sauce, rice vinegar, and chili crisp to a bowl. Then I add the wontons and gently swirl them in the sauce.

PART 2:
CELEBRATING OUR MIXED CULTURE

Our year of celebrations also includes non-Chinese holidays such as Easter, Thanksgiving, Christmas, and July 4th. We make the foods traditional to those holidays and also include a Chinese touch via stir-fries that act as side dishes. We also have hybrid birthday celebrations that nod to our mixed cultures.

Birthdays and Party Bites

Long-Life Noodles or Chocolate Cake?

BIRTHDAYS AND PARTY BITES RECIPES

MIXING IT UP FOR BIRTHDAYS AND OTHER PARTIES

生日快樂!

Shēngrì kuàilè!

Happy birthday!

We're pretty Americanized when it comes to birthdays. We usually go out and the birthday person gets to pick where we eat. Sometimes it's burgers or pizza, and other times it's omakase sushi or soup dumplings. There's always a birthday cake, usually chocolate, either from one of our favorite bakeries or homemade from Alice Medrich's book *Sinfully Easy Delicious Desserts* (the one-bowl chocolate cake recipe is delicious and foolproof).

When the kids were little, we'd have parties with groups of their classmates and send them home with treat bags. (Speaking of treat bags, what a racket! After a few times dropping too much money on cheap doodads and "throwaway" toys, we quit the practice.) As the kids got older, they each would get the choice to have an afternoon party at the house with lots of friends and family or pick two or three friends and go do dinner and an activity. For her eleventh birthday, Meilee got to go out with a friend for manicures and dinner at a favorite Vietnamese restaurant, capped with a ride in the "Seattle Car Karaoke" Lyft to get ice cream. The girls sat in the back seat and sang a few songs and then got to sign the hood of the car (the driver asked all his guests to sign his car). Shen has chosen to attend baseball games with a small group of friends and eat whatever they want at the stadium.

Back when the Space Needle had a rotating restaurant, both kids got to go with friends for their eighth birthdays to have dinner and get the Lunar Orbiter dessert, which is a brownie sundae that arrives in dramatic fashion in a dry-ice bowl with a trail of fog. The tradition at the restaurant was to place a birthday card on the windowsill by your table. As the restaurant rotated and other diners passed the card, they would sign it. By the time the restaurant made a full revolution, you'd get the card back filled with well wishes from people from all over the world who were visiting Seattle and the Space Needle. Meilee even got a signature from a former Seahawks football player who happened to be at the restaurant with his family.

But for Lau Lau, Meilee's grandma Ellen Chou, we swing back to our roots and have a Chinese meal either at a restaurant or at home. She follows the traditional Chinese calendar when it comes to her birthday, so it's on a different day every year. We have to check the calendar every spring to know when her day is. As our matriarch has gotten older, she tends to prefer familiar flavors that agree more with her body constitution. Western food tends to have more dairy (butter, cheese, yogurt, cream), which is too intense for her. But we all, of course, love our big family dinners at any number of Chinese restaurants. It might be soup dumplings or dim sum or Sichuan food or hot pot. We've come together to celebrate her seventieth, seventy-fifth, and now her eighties. It's a privilege to be able to bring together three generations around the table to pay our respects and share our favorite dishes.

It's customary to eat a bowl of long-life noodles on birthdays as a wish for longevity. It's not a specific recipe but the symbolism of eating long strands of noodles. We might have stir-fried noodles or soup noodles, and within those two methods of cooking, there's an infinite range of flavors and components that might accompany the dish. A family favorite is Taiwanese red-braised beef noodle soup. We braise beef shank until the broth is rich and the meat is tender and caramelized. (That recipe is in *Chinese Soul Food*.) We also love noodles in chicken broth (page 174), which soothes with hints of ginger and green onions and the umami of shiitake mushrooms.

Lau Lau likes the Chinese-bakery-style cake with fresh fruit. This is a white cake with whipped cream and assorted fresh fruit. This can be really great when the fruits make sense. What do we mean? Well, let's just say that some Asian bakeries like to include fruits that don't quite match the texture of cake, and when you try to take a forkful, you end up destroying the cake. For example, one year, the cake from the bakery—unbeknownst to us—contained honeydew, cantaloupe, and whole grapes in the middle. This is where we laugh out loud at the image of us trying to slice such a cake into neat wedges. It was not pretty and it wasn't pleasant

Meilee made the cake for Shen's birthday and used fondant and everything.

生
日
宴
：
長
壽
麵
？
巧
克
力
蛋
糕
？

to eat. We attribute this to two truths: Baked cakes—desserts in general—aren't a part of our culture in the same way that they are in many Western countries that have deep histories with the anatomy of a layer cake. The other truth is that a plate of cut fruit or a bunch of fresh lychee is what we typically serve as a last bite.

Melon cakes aside, a Chinese bakery cake can be delicate and light. When we've made them at home for Lau Lau's birthday, we choose assorted berries, stone fruits, or mangoes—soft-fleshed fruits that won't surprise your palate. Lau Lau

is always delighted no matter what the cake is; she's happy being surrounded by her three adult children and her seven grandkids.

The recipes in this chapter acknowledge the customary long-life noodles for birthdays. But the rest of the recipes reflect party foods that are crowd-friendly. It's a party—we're going to enjoy quality time with some fried foods, wings, and cake.

Meilee celebrated her eighth birthday at the Space Needle when it still had a revolving restaurant.

We made a fruit-filled sponge cake for Lau Lau's eightieth birthday.

171

MEILEE'S PERSPECTIVE: WHAT'S IN A BIRTH NAME?

I often ponder the significance of the two syllables that have followed me through life, whispered by loved ones, called out in moments of joy and frustration, and etched onto countless documents. Although my name may seem like a simple combination of letters, *Meilee* holds within it a world of identity, emotion, and a lifetime of stories waiting to be told.

To truly grasp the importance of a name, you must recognize that names are more than just labels. They are threads connecting us to our roots, our heritage, and the values of our parents and ancestors. In my family, names all have important meanings that represent us and our character.

My brother's name is Shen. *Shen* means "deep thinker." My mom wanted to name him that so he would always remember to think through the consequences of his actions. As an energetic teenage boy, I think that is now more important than ever. He just started his freshman year of high school (2023). My hope is that he will reflect on his name's meaning and make smart decisions in these very chaotic next four years.

Names have a peculiar way of shaping our perceptions and expectations. A name can elicit a sense of belonging and cultural pride, or remind us of our family's triumphs and tribulations.

As for my name, Meilee 玫力, in Mandarin, the character 玫 (*mei*) translates to "rose"—a symbol of beauty, grace, and timeless elegance. When my mom chose this name for me, she was drawn to the symbolism of the rose. She admired how this flower embodies the power of gentleness and refinement in a world often marred by chaos and conflict. My name reminds me that beauty can flourish and inspire even in the harshest environments.

The character 力 (*li*) translates to "strength" or "force" (though the pinyin spelling is "lì," my mom decided to spell my name Meilee with the *lee* to make it easier for people to *attempt* to say). Like a rose covered with thorns, my name is a testament to resilience and grit. These thorns are not meant to make me prickly; instead, they give me the means to defend myself and navigate the world's complexities. My mom's choice was not merely a matter of aesthetics of language; it was a deliberate decision to equip me with the inherent traits necessary to thrive in a society that all too often questions the worth and potential of women and individuals of color. Each stroke of *lee* overflows with determination and promises that I will survive and thrive in the face of adversity.

Mei, or the rose, has been a guiding light during my high school years. Despite the emotional turmoil that accompanied these times, I learned to appreciate the small wonders within myself and my surroundings. Coping with depression, anxiety, and anorexia was a taxing journey that often felt overwhelming. I believed life had pushed me to the point of no return. That was until I discovered the beauty of resilience and recovery. Just as a rose can weather storms and bloom gracefully, I overcame my mental health challenges, emerging from the darkness with a newfound appreciation for the beauty of simplicity and choosing life.

Lee, or strength, has been my constant companion throughout life's challenges. I remember my grade school years, when I encountered prejudice and stereotypes because of my mixed-race background.

It was Lunar New Year in first grade. It was a cherished day at home, marked by red decorations adorning the walls and an array of delectable dishes for an evening feast. However, the magic quickly dissipated once I arrived at school. I got laughed at and teased while trying to share this celebration with my classmates. I became hesitant to wear my qipao to school, even on Lunar New Year, out of fear and a desire to conform. It seemed as though I needed to erase a significant part of my identity to blend in.

Despite that, I was constantly dealing with being stereotyped based on my appearance and having to explain and defend my identity to those who were quick to make assumptions. During those moments, I embraced the resilience embedded within my name. Like the thorns protecting a rose, I used my strength not to build walls but to break down barriers and challenge preconceptions. *Lee* gave me the fortitude to speak out against injustice and to empower others who faced similar struggles. It became a source of empowerment, propelling me to pursue my passions and advocate for positive change.

Meilee is not just my name. It reflects my journey to becoming the person I am today and is a celebration of the beauty and strength within me. Through navigating my mixed-race identity and passions of advocacy and creativity, I have weaved the threads together to create a narrative that is mine—a narrative that lives out the true meaning of Meilee.

幸
福
饗
宴

雞絲青菜炒麵條
STIR-FRIED LONG-LIFE NOODLES
with Chicken and Vegetables

EFFORT ●○○

MAKES 4 SERVINGS, FAMILY STYLE

8 ounces chicken breast

3 tablespoons soy sauce, divided

2 teaspoons cornstarch

2 tablespoons vegetable oil, divided

12 ounces dried Chinese noodles

2 tablespoons water

1 tablespoon hoisin sauce

1 teaspoon minced fresh ginger

1 green onion, chopped

2 cloves garlic, minced or crushed

½ cup julienned carrots

½ cup mushrooms, such as shimeji or enoki, segmented

3 cups sliced greens, such as baby bok choy or Chinese cabbage

½ teaspoon sesame oil

Kosher salt, if needed

Eating noodles on your birthday comes with a wish for a long life. So it's important that you never cut or break the noodles. If you ever make noodles from scratch, you can pull or roll out extra-long noodles. There's flexibility to the vegetables, protein, and sauce flavors you can use, so feel free to riff on this basic recipe.

■ Cut the chicken breast lengthwise into two to three strips, about 1½ inches wide, or about the size of chicken tenders. Then slice each strip of chicken crosswise into slivers. The exact size of the slivers is not as important as keeping the pieces relatively uniform. In a small bowl, combine the chicken with 1 tablespoon of the soy sauce and mix well. Add the cornstarch and mix well again.

■ Preheat a wok over high heat until wisps of smoke rise from the surface. Add 1 tablespoon of the vegetable oil and heat until it starts to shimmer. Add the chicken and, using a spatula, quickly spread it into a single layer in the bowl of the wok. After about 15 seconds, stir-fry the chicken for about 1 more minute, or until it is nearly cooked through. Remove the wok from the heat, transfer the chicken to a small bowl, and set aside. Rinse the wok and dry with a towel.

■ Bring a large pot of water to boil over high heat. Add the noodles and cook for 9 to 11 minutes, or until they are soft but not mushy. The cooking time will depend on the thickness of the noodles. Check the instructions on the package for reference. When the noodles are done, drain them and set aside.

■ While the noodles cook, prepare the sauce ingredients. In a small bowl, combine the remaining 2 tablespoons soy sauce, water, hoisin sauce, ginger, green onions, and garlic. Stir to combine and set aside.

■ Preheat a wok over high heat until wisps of smoke rise from the surface. Add the remaining 1 tablespoon vegetable oil and heat for a few seconds until it starts to shimmer. Add the carrots, mushrooms, and greens. Stir-fry for about 1 minute, or until the crisp vegetables begin to soften. Add the chicken and stir to combine. Add the noodles and the sauce and stir to combine. You may need to use a pair of tongs and the wok spatula to help maneuver the noodles. If the sauce looks like it's cooking down too fast, reduce the heat to medium. Continue to toss ingredients together to make sure the sauce coats the noodles. Drizzle with the sesame oil. Turn off the heat. Taste a bite of noodles. If needed, add salt to taste and toss again. Transfer to a serving dish.

MOM SAYS: This dish works for a lot of personal preferences. You can use any protein or use tofu and keep it vegetarian. You can make it spicy by adding hot sauce or chili crisp. You can add a handful of fresh bean sprouts at the end to add some crunch.

幸
福
饗
宴

長壽湯麵
LONG-LIFE NOODLES IN BROTH

EFFORT ● ● ○

MAKES 4 TO 6 SERVINGS, FAMILY STYLE

1½ quarts Chinese-Style Chicken Broth (page 226)

1 slice fresh ginger, about ¼ inch thick and 2 inches long

1 green onion, cut into 2-inch segments

Kosher salt

2 cups sliced baby bok choy, Chinese cabbage, or leafy green of choice

12 ounces dried Chinese noodles

Sesame oil, for serving

Chopped fresh cilantro, fried shallots, chili sauce, or chili crisp, for garnish (optional)

Noodles in broth is a soothing dish and, on birthdays, brings with it a wish for longevity. Don't cut or break the noodles or you might sever the good wishes. While we like chicken broth, you could use vegetable broth. Try different widths of noodles or use fresh noodles, if you have access to an Asian market. Feel free to add other vegetables, including carrots, mushrooms, sprouts, and such.

■ Bring a large pot of water to boil to cook the noodles. Separately, in a 4-quart pot over high heat, add the broth, ginger, and green onions. Bring to a boil and reduce heat to medium-low. Taste for seasoning and add salt to taste. Add the bok choy and let simmer in the broth. The goal is to cook the vegetables so they're no longer raw, but you don't want to overcook them. So keep watch and reduce the heat to low as needed.

■ When the large pot of water comes to a boil, add the dried noodles and cook for 9 to 11 minutes, or according to the instructions on the box. The noodles should be tender but not mushy. When cooked, drain the noodles. Portion into bowls.

■ Ladle the broth and vegetables over the noodles. Add a few drops of sesame oil to each bowl. Add garnishes and serve.

> **MOM SAYS:** Homemade broth is best if you have the time to make it in advance. If you use a store-bought chicken broth, it's likely to be one that was made with "American" flavors. I doctor the flavor by adding ginger, onions, and dried shiitake mushrooms, and letting it simmer for a bit. I may also add a splash of Shaoxing wine. This shifts the flavor profile and adds that umami kick.

幸
福
饗
宴

辣味脆皮豆腐
TOFU POPPERS
with Chili Crisp

VEGETARIAN

EFFORT ●●○

MAKES 4 SERVINGS, FAMILY STYLE

Vegetable oil, for frying

1 cup cornstarch, for dredging

2 (8-ounce) tubes of egg tofu, carefully removed and sliced ¾ inch thick, or 1 (14- to 16-ounce) package soft tofu, cut into 1-inch cubes

1 teaspoon kosher salt, plus more as needed

Chili crisp, such as Fly By Jing, Kari Kari, or your preferred brand, for garnish

Chopped fresh cilantro, for garnish (optional)

Egg tofu is what it suggests: tofu that's made with egg in it. It has a delicate custard-like texture and is sold in clear tubes. You cut the tube open carefully and shimmy the tofu out of the casing. After frying, the coating becomes lightly crisp and the inside remains tender. But if you can't find egg tofu or fear that it might be too delicate to work with, you certainly can use regular soft or medium-firm tofu.

■ In a 4-quart Dutch oven or a deep-sided skillet, add vegetable oil to a depth of about ¾ inch. Heat over medium heat to 350 degrees F.

■ Meanwhile, place the cornstarch in a medium bowl or on a dinner plate. Place several pieces of tofu in the cornstarch and coat evenly. Check the temperature of the oil. Using a spatula (or similar tool that can help you place the tofu in the oil), add several pieces of dredged tofu to the oil. Don't overcrowd the pot. Fry the tofu pieces for about 1 minute on each side, or until lightly golden. When done, transfer to a small baking tray or large plate lined with paper towels. Repeat with the remaining tofu.

■ To serve, arrange the fried tofu on a serving dish and sprinkle with salt. Drizzle chili crisp over the tofu. Top with cilantro. Serve while hot.

MOM SAYS: While you do want to eat these tofu poppers hot, be mindful that they can burn your taste buds if you eat them straight out of the oil. I have been too eager in the past and suffered the consequences.

Broccoli has so much more life when it's charred and stir-fried with garlic and soy sauce. This is a straightforward way to make broccoli that delivers more punch than your guests might expect. It's a favorite for the broccoli-loving members of our family.

焗鍋蒜味綠菜花
WOK-CHARRED GARLIC BROCCOLI

VEGAN

EFFORT ●○○

MAKES 4 SERVINGS, FAMILY STYLE

■ Preheat the wok over high heat until wisps of smoke rise from the surface. Swirl in the oil and heat for a few seconds until it starts to shimmer. Add the broccoli and spread into a single layer in the wok. Let sear for about 15 seconds or so. Stir-fry for a few seconds and let sear for about 10 seconds more. Add the water and cover with a lid. Let the broccoli steam for about 30 seconds. Remove the lid, add the soy sauce and garlic, and stir-fry for about 1 minute. Drizzle with the sesame oil and transfer to a serving dish. Sprinkle on the fried garlic or fried shallots.

1 tablespoon vegetable oil

12 ounces broccoli crowns, cut into bite-size florets

3 tablespoons water

1½ tablespoons soy sauce

2 cloves garlic, crushed

½ teaspoon sesame oil

1 tablespoon fried garlic or fried shallots (optional)

MOM SAYS: Look for fried garlic and fried shallots at Asian markets. They're useful to keep in the pantry for adding crunch and savoriness to a simple dish such as wok-charred broccoli.

Baby bok choy is available everywhere, it seems. It can accompany so many other ingredients, but it holds its own as the star in this dish. Look for small baby bok choy versus the large, overgrown ones (read more on page 22). If you want to try the Asian-style jarred garlic, this is a dish that will allow you to experiment. The minced garlic in the jar is definitely more pungent, so fair warning. Of course, fresh garlic is always a great choice.

■ Trim the baby bok choy: Slice about ½ inch off the stem end. Then cut each head of baby bok choy in half lengthwise through the core. Make diagonal cuts around the core to remove it. Once the core is out, the leaves should separate. Rinse in cool water and shake dry. Slice the bok choy roughly into 1-inch segments. Set aside.

■ Preheat a wok over high heat until wisps of smoke rise from the surface. Swirl in the vegetable oil and let heat for a few seconds until it starts to shimmer. Add the bok choy and stir-fry for about 1 minute. Add the garlic and soy sauce. Stir-fry for 1 to 2 minutes, making sure the garlic gets evenly distributed. Add the sesame oil and the white pepper. Toss one last time and then transfer to a serving dish.

> **MOM SAYS:** If you can get to a well-stocked Asian market, you sometimes can find "bok choy mui," which is the tiny baby bok choy that are 3 to 4 inches long. With these, you can separate the leaves by plucking them from the core. Cook the leaves whole. This doesn't work for heads of bok choy that are longer than that, however.

蒜味小白菜
SUPER-GARLICKY BABY BOK CHOY

VEGAN

EFFORT ●○○

MAKES 4 SERVINGS, FAMILY STYLE

12 ounces baby bok choy

1 tablespoon vegetable oil

4 large cloves garlic, thinly sliced, or 1 teaspoon or more jarred garlic

1½ tablespoons soy sauce

½ teaspoon sesame oil

⅛ teaspoon white pepper powder (optional)

生
日
宴
：
長
壽
麵
？
巧
克
力
蛋
糕
？

This is an approachable way to make ribs that yields lip-smacking flavor. We usually use riblets, but the recipe works well with baby back ribs too. It's important to watch the cooking toward the end. The liquid will gradually reduce and the sauce will become very thick and sticky.

糖醋小排
SWEET-AND-SOUR BABY BACK RIBS

EFFORT ●○○

MAKES 4 TO 6 SERVINGS, FAMILY STYLE

1 rack baby back ribs (about 2 pounds)

4 cups water

½ cup soy sauce

¼ cup Chinese black vinegar or balsamic vinegar

¼ cup rock sugar or dark brown sugar

¼ cup Shaoxing wine

6 cloves garlic, lightly smashed and peeled

3 green onions, cut into 2-inch segments, plus more for garnish

■ Cut the rack into individual ribs. Place in a large Dutch oven with the water, making sure the ribs are covered. If needed, adjust the water amount. Bring to a boil over high heat, then reduce the heat to medium-low. Let simmer for about 15 minutes; use a fine-mesh skimmer to remove the scum that floats to the surface. Repeat this step as needed during this initial simmer time.

■ Reduce the heat to low. Add the soy sauce, vinegar, sugar, wine, garlic, and green onions. Stir to distribute. Let simmer for 30 to 45 minutes.

■ At the 30-minute mark, use a fork on the largest rib to check tenderness. If the fork struggles, then continue to simmer, shifting ribs around as needed to make sure the larger ribs remain in contact with the liquid. After another 10 to 15 minutes, check for tenderness again. When the ribs are tender, it's time to finish the sauce. Turn the heat up to medium-high and let the sauce reduce, stirring occasionally, for up to 15 minutes, or until the consistency is thick and syrupy. Turn off the heat. Transfer the ribs to a platter and use a large rubber spatula to scoop the sauce out and onto the ribs. Add some green onion slivers on top for garnish.

MOM SAYS: Reducing the sauce can be tricky. Sometimes, the ribs become so tender that they start to fall off the bone. If that's the case and you still need to reduce the sauce, take the ribs out and set aside. Then turn up the heat to reduce the sauce to the point where it's starting to turn syrupy. Add the ribs back in and roll them around to coat. Remove from the heat and serve.

幸
福
饗
宴

炸雞球

POPCORN CHICKEN

EFFORT ●●○

MAKES 4 SERVINGS, FAMILY STYLE

1 pound boneless, skin-on chicken thighs, cut into 1-inch chunks

1½ tablespoons soy sauce

1 tablespoon hoisin sauce

2 cups cornstarch

¼ teaspoon five-spice powder

2 teaspoons kosher salt, divided

¼ teaspoon white pepper powder

Vegetable oil, for frying

Handful of fresh basil leaves

Fried chicken in any form is a winner in our family. The beauty of popcorn chicken is that it fries quickly and, because the pieces are bite-size, it doesn't take long for the flavors to sink in. Traditionally, the dredge is made of tapioca or potato starch. We found that cornstarch works well too, and is definitely more widely available.

■ Place the chicken in a large bowl. Add the soy sauce and hoisin sauce. Mix well with the chicken to coat. Let marinate for about 10 minutes.

■ Meanwhile, place the cornstarch on a dinner plate or in a medium bowl. Set aside. Make the dipping salts: Combine the five-spice powder with 1 teaspoon of the kosher salt in a small pinch bowl. Separately, combine the remaining 1 teaspoon kosher salt with the white pepper in a small pinch bowl. Set aside for dipping. Line a plate with paper towels and set aside.

■ In a 4-quart pot, add vegetable oil to a depth of 1½ inches and heat over medium heat to 350 degrees F. Add the chicken in batches to the cornstarch and roll around to coat well. Gently shake off any loose starch and place the chicken in the oil. Fry for 2 to 3 minutes, or until lightly golden, stirring occasionally so the chicken cooks evenly. Transfer the chicken with a slotted spoon to the dinner plate lined with paper towels. Repeat with the remaining chicken. When you have about 1 minute left in the cooking time for the last batch of chicken, drop the basil leaves into the oil. Transfer the chicken and basil leaves to a serving platter. Serve with the dipping salts.

> **MOM SAYS:** If you have some food picks or toothpicks, you can plant a few in the chicken so people can pick up the chicken easily. My son, Shen, always likes to dip the chicken in sweet chili sauce, so feel free to use the condiment of your choice.

幸
福
饗
宴

紅燒雞翅
SAUCY CHICKEN WINGS

EFFORT ●●○

MAKES 4 TO 6 APPETIZER SERVINGS

1½ pounds chicken wing flats, or flats and drumettes

1 teaspoon grated fresh ginger

2 green onions, finely chopped

4 to 6 cloves garlic, crushed

1 cup dark brown sugar

¾ cup water

½ cup soy sauce

¼ cup white vinegar

2 tablespoons cornstarch

Chicken wings in a savory-sweet sauce are a great party food. Everyone loves the sauce and pours it on rice. We prefer the wing flats, but you can use flats and drumettes or just drumettes.

■ Preheat the oven to 425 degrees F. Line a baking sheet with parchment paper. Place the chicken wings in a single layer on the sheet pan. Bake for 20 to 30 minutes, or until the thickest wing reaches an internal temperature of 160 degrees F.

■ Meanwhile, in a 4-quart pot, combine the ginger, green onions, garlic, brown sugar, water, soy sauce, and vinegar. Bring to a simmer over medium heat, stirring to dissolve the sugar. Let simmer for 5 minutes. Carefully take a small taste. If it's too salty or sweet, add a smidge of water.

■ In a small bowl, mix the cornstarch with 2 tablespoons water, then drizzle into the sauce and stir to combine. Let simmer for 1 minute more, then turn off the heat. When the wings are done, add to the sauce and stir to coat. Transfer to a platter and serve.

MOM SAYS: Ideally, you would deep-fry the wings before adding them to the sauce. But that gets super messy. If you have an air fryer, you can use that to get some crispy edges on the wings.

生
日
宴
：
長
壽
麵
？
巧
克
力
蛋
糕
？

Also known as crab Rangoon, these creamy wontons are a throwback to Trader Vic's Polynesian restaurant chain. It's very much an Americanized appetizer that's fun for parties. You can easily double the filling recipe since a pack of wonton wrappers has more than twenty pieces.

蟹角
CREAM CHEESE WONTONS
with Crab

EFFORT ●○○
MAKES ABOUT 20 WONTONS

1 (8-ounce) package cream cheese (regular and not whipped)

¼ cup cooked crab meat

½ teaspoon kosher salt

⅛ teaspoon white pepper powder

1 package wonton wrappers

Vegetable oil, for frying

Sweet-and-Sour Sauce (recipe follows) or store-bought sweet chili sauce, for dipping

■ In a medium bowl, combine the cream cheese, crab, salt, and white pepper. Mix well.

■ Line a baking sheet with parchment paper. Place about 1 tablespoon of filling in the middle of a wonton wrapper. Take the midpoint of each side of the wonton square and, in turn, press it into the filling at the center. What you'll get is a shape that has four "spires" at each corner. The cheese acts like glue to keep the wonton sealed in the center. Repeat with the remaining filling. You will probably have leftover wonton wrappers, which you can wrap in a ziplock bag and freeze for next time.

■ In a 4-quart Dutch oven (or similar), add oil to a depth of about 3 inches. Heat over medium heat to 350 degrees F. Fry the wontons in batches for 1 to 2 minutes, or just until golden. Transfer to a platter lined with paper towels. Repeat with the remaining wontons. Let cool for about 1 minute and eat while still warm and creamy. Serve with Sweet-and-Sour Sauce or sweet chili sauce. ⟶

MOM SAYS: In many takeout restaurants, they use imitation crab (surimi) in these wontons. You certainly could use that product, if you'd like, but it does taste better with real crab. You also can skip the crab altogether and just use cream cheese.

Sweet-and-Sour Sauce

VEGAN
EFFORT ●○○
MAKES ABOUT 1 CUP

½ cup sugar

⅓ cup ketchup

⅓ cup white vinegar

You can buy sweet-and-sour sauce from the store, of course. This is a simple recipe you can throw together with ingredients you likely already have.

■ In a small pot over medium heat, combine the sugar, ketchup, and vinegar. Stir until the sugar dissolves and the sauce becomes syrupy, 5 to 7 minutes. Let cool and serve.

MOM SAYS: This is the sweet-and-sour sauce that we served in my family's Chinese restaurant, which was in business from 1980 to 2003 in Columbia, Missouri. At the restaurant, we added a thickener. I skipped that step for this version.

生
日
宴
：
長
壽
麵
？
巧
克
力
蛋
糕
？

We don't make these often, which means that when we do, they taste especially good. You can swap the pork and shrimp with chicken, if you'd like. Or, if you have a shellfish allergy, you can skip the shrimp and use more pork. The filling is flexible, but aim for about a pound of protein total. There are different ways to fold the wontons too, so if you grew up doing it differently, no problem. Fold them the way you know how!

■ Cut the shrimp into fine dice and place in a large bowl. Add the ground pork, green onions, soy sauce, ginger, sesame oil, and white pepper. Mix well.

■ Line a baking sheet with parchment paper. Place ¼ cup water in a small bowl. Place a flat teaspoon's amount of filling at the center of a wonton wrapper. Dip your finger in the water and drag it along one edge of the wonton wrapper and repeat with all four sides. Fold the wrapper in half over the filling, lining up the edges and pressing down to seal. You will have a rectangular packet. Hold the rectangle with the fold side down. Now dip your finger in the water again and dab it on the underside of the right corner of the rectangle. Maneuver the wonton and bend it so that the right corner, the one you've just dabbed with water, overlaps with the left corner. Press together to seal. Place on the parchment-lined tray. Repeat with the remaining filling and wonton wrappers, then line them up in columns to optimize the space on the tray.

■ In a 4-quart Dutch oven (or similar), add oil to a depth of about 1½ inches. Heat over medium heat to 350 degrees F. Fry the wontons in batches for 2 to 3 minutes, or just until golden. Transfer to a platter lined with paper towels. Repeat with remaining wontons. Serve with Sweet-and-Sour Sauce or store-bought sweet chili sauce.

> **MOM SAYS:** In Asian markets, you can get ground pork that contains marbling (a.k.a. fat). It's similar to how ground beef is sold with different fat content. The marbling provides flavor and helps to keep the filling from being dry. If you can't get to an Asian market, look for unseasoned bulk sausage mix at your grocery store.

炸餛吞 (豬肉鮮蝦)
PORK AND SHRIMP FRIED WONTONS

EFFORT ●●○
MAKES ABOUT 40 WONTONS

4 ounces peeled and deveined fresh shrimp

12 ounces ground pork

2 green onions, finely chopped

1 tablespoon soy sauce

1 teaspoon grated fresh ginger

½ teaspoon sesame oil

⅛ teaspoon white pepper powder

1 package wonton wrappers

Vegetable oil, for frying

Sweet-and-Sour Sauce (page 188) or store-bought sweet chili sauce, for dipping

Cupcakes are great for parties because you don't need a fork, and you may not even need a plate. The fruit you choose should be in season for the best flavor and have similar textures. Be sure to cut the fruit pieces into shapes that are easy to eat.

- Preheat the oven to 350 degrees F. Line a muffin tin with cupcake liners and set aside.

- In a medium bowl, whip the egg whites using an electric mixer until soft peaks form. Gradually add ¼ cup of the sugar while continuing to whip until stiff peaks form. Set aside.

- In a large bowl, whisk the egg yolks with the remaining ¼ cup sugar until well combined and slightly thickened. Mix the vegetable oil, milk, and vanilla extract into the egg yolk mixture. Set aside.

- In another medium bowl, sift together the cake flour, baking powder, and salt. Gently fold the sifted dry ingredients into the egg yolk mixture until fully combined. Carefully fold in about a third of the whipped egg whites to lighten the batter. Then gently fold in the remaining egg whites until no streaks remain. Be very gentle so you don't deflate the batter.

- Divide the batter among the cake cups, filling them about two-thirds full. Bake the cupcakes for 15 to 18 minutes, or until a toothpick inserted into the center comes out clean or with just a few moist crumbs. Remove the cupcakes from the oven and let them cool in the muffin tin for a few minutes, then transfer them to a wire rack to cool completely. ⟶

中式口味水果杯子蛋糕
CHINESE-BAKERY-INSPIRED CUPCAKES
with Fruit

生日宴：長壽麵？巧克力蛋糕？

VEGETARIAN
EFFORT ●●●
MAKES 12 CUPCAKES

FOR THE CAKE:

3 large eggs, separated

½ cup (100 grams) granulated sugar, divided

¼ cup vegetable oil

¼ cup milk

½ teaspoon vanilla extract

¾ cup (100 grams) cake flour

1 teaspoon baking powder

¼ teaspoon salt

FOR THE FROSTING:

2 cups heavy whipping cream, chilled

⅓ cup mascarpone cheese

¼ cup confectioners' sugar

1 teaspoon vanilla extract

Fresh fruit, such as assorted fresh berries, mango, peach, for garnish

- In the meantime, make the frosting. Add the heavy cream, mascarpone, confectioners' sugar, and vanilla to the bowl of a stand mixer (or a large mixing bowl if you're using a hand mixer) and whisk on medium-high speed for about 2 minutes, or until stiff peaks form. Refrigerate until ready to decorate.

- Prepare your choice of fruit for decorating the cakes.

- Once the cupcakes are cool, add a dollop of whipped cream and arrange the fresh fruit on top. Alternatively, you can pipe the whipped cream to get a prettier design.

MOM SAYS: You can use multicolored cupcake liners to add a pop of color. For the cupcakes in the photo, I sliced strawberries and used a mini cutter to stamp mango flowers. The rainbow sprinkles were an extra touch to make the photo look fun. If I were making this for my mother, I'd leave off the sprinkles because she prefers fruit only.

Stir-Fries Make Great Holiday Side Dishes

STIR-FRIED RECIPES

If you need some ideas for how to choose a side dish for major Western holidays, below are some suggested pairings.

Of course, these are just suggestions. You may want to bring appetizers instead of a side dish. If that's the case, you might pop over to the Birthdays and Party Bites chapter (page 168) to explore some fried-and-yummy appetizers. Note that, depending on the size of the party, you may want to double the recipe you choose.

EASTER HAM

Dry-Fried Green Beans (page 202)

Stir-Fried Escarole with Shiitake (page 213)

Chinese Chives with Mushrooms (page 203)

JULY 4TH BARBECUE

Stir-Fried Shoestring Potatoes (page 218)

Dry-Fried Okra with Chilies and Goji (page 200)

Hot-and-Sour Taiwanese Cabbage (page 216)

THANKSGIVING TURKEY

Wok-Charred Brussels Sprouts with Smoked Soy Sauce (page 205)

Stir-Fried Kale with Dried Cranberries (page 214)

Dry-Fried Green Beans (page 202)

VEGAN THANKSGIVING

Braised Daikon (page 210)

Garlic Eggplant (page 206)

Stir-Fried Kale with Dried Cranberries (page 214)

CHRISTMAS ROAST

Chinese Chives with Mushrooms (page 203)

Stir-Fried Escarole with Shiitake (page 213)

Dry-Fried Green Beans (page 202)

CHRISTMAS DUCK

Braised Chinese Cabbage (page 209)

Garlic Eggplant (page 206)

Chinese Chives with Mushrooms (page 203)

MEILEE'S PERSPECTIVE: WHAT'S CULTURE WHEN YOU'RE MIXED-RACE?

Growing up as a mixed-race teenager is an experience that shares both good sides and bad. The fusion of cultures within one person's identity is complex and creates a mosaic of traditions, languages, and perspectives that really help form who we are. I love being Chinese American and I am very proud of my culture, every part of it.

The struggle I think that many mixed-race people can sympathize with is the constant feeling of having to choose one side of your cultural identity. The pressure of having to pick sometimes starts to get to you. Maybe I am not Chinese enough? Maybe I am too Chinese-y. It's a never-ending loop.

In grade school, I was one of three Asian kids in my class. We were all mixed, and despite the half-white we had in common with the rest of our classmates, we felt like outsiders. I spent a lot of my life having to constantly question my identity—will I ever be enough?

I've talked about Lunar New Year being just another day for classmates (see page 52). We didn't get a day off school, and only two of three kids in the class were celebrating, so it didn't really matter to anyone. I continued my day, because even then I was used to feeling alone, and I tried not to let it bother me. I never wore my qipao to school, even on Lunar New Year, out of fear. I wanted to blend in and be accepted, but in order to do that, it felt like I had to erase such a big part of me to fit in. I can't erase the parts of my culture that are physically a part of me; always dealing with the burden of being stereotyped based on my appearance and having

to explain and defend my identity to those who are quick to make assumptions.

However, amid the challenges, there are stories of resilience and moments of self-discovery.

I joined the Asian Student Union (ASU) my freshman year of high school. I was able to meet so many mixed-race kids. I had finally found a place where being me was enough. I was Meilee and that was all I needed to be. Due to COVID-19, all of the meetings that year were held over Zoom. Despite everything, I was still able to find support, especially during a time when we all needed it, given the relentless racism surrounding the pandemic.

The following year, ASU was back in person. We gathered in a big room in the library, all sitting in a circle, and we just talked. Our conversations ranged from our experiences at a predominantly white high school to going back into history and learning about the model minority myth and Asian representation. I loved the environment; it was safe and relatable. I never had to explain any nuances of my identity—people understood who I was and how I was feeling. It all felt like I was reviving this part of my culture I had neglected for so long.

One of my favorite memories from ASU was our potluck. My mom helped me make dumplings to bring to the potluck. There were dozens of different kinds of dumplings spread across the table alongside colorful side dishes and of course a rice cooker at the end. It brought us all a lot closer and created a connection through food that we all appreciated, no matter where we were from. It was really cool to see how all these traditions were not confined to a single way of doing things.

As I look forward, I am hopeful that society will continue to evolve in its understanding and acceptance of mixed-race people. I hope to see a world where assumptions based on appearance are replaced by genuine curiosity and appreciation for the incredible diversity of human backgrounds.

All in all, growing up as a mixed-race person is an extraordinary journey. I've learned to not only accept but embrace the complexity and nuances of my identity, and I have gained so much strength and confidence from it. To anyone mixed-race or not, exploring your identity is a great adventure that gives you a huge opportunity to establish a deeper connection with yourself and your ancestors. So, as our society continues to grow and become more diverse, let my experience as a mixed-race teen serve as a reminder that our differences are what bring us together and make us human.

Mom Says: Everyone Loves Dry-Fried Green Beans

When it's time for Thanksgiving, Christmas, Easter, or other major Western holidays involving a meal that includes side dishes, we get requests for Dry-Fried Green Beans (page 202). The way we make it—with blistered beans, scallions, ginger, garlic, and soy sauce that caramelizes with a touch of sugar—is not how members of our extended non-Chinese family grew up with green beans. It was a revelation to them that green beans could be so savory and delicious. So, for twenty years, when we've gone to Grandma Linda's home for a holiday, we have to bring Dry-Fried Green Beans. But green beans aren't the only vegetable stir-fry that can help transform slices of ham or turkey. Stir-Fried Kale with Dried Cranberries (page 214) or Wok-Charred Brussels Sprouts with Smoked Soy Sauce (page 205) would be fantastic in either scenario. They might even steal the show.

幸
福
饗
宴

乾燒秋葵＋枸杞
DRY-FRIED OKRA
with Chilies and Goji

VEGAN
EFFORT ●○○
MAKES 4 SERVINGS, FAMILY STYLE

¾ to 1 pound fresh whole okra (small pods)

Vegetable oil, for frying

1 green onion, finely chopped

1 teaspoon finely minced or grated fresh ginger

1 large clove garlic, crushed or finely minced

3 to 4 dried red chilies

2 tablespoons dried goji berries (optional)

1½ tablespoons soy sauce

1 teaspoon sugar

½ teaspoon sesame oil

A dear family friend experimented with growing okra, and it inspired us to think about different ways to use the bounty. The dry-fried method we use for beans works perfectly for okra. Be sure to buy the freshest okra that are still small. If they're overgrown, they'll have a tough texture and won't be pleasant to eat.

■ Trim the stems off the okra, leaving a thin layer of the stem at the top so that the okra pod remains sealed. Line a dinner plate or a large bowl with two layers of paper towels. Set aside.

■ In a 4-quart Dutch oven or similar, add vegetable oil to a depth of 1 inch. Heat on medium to 350 degrees F. In batches, add the okra and fry for about 30 seconds, or until the outer surface starts to blister. Use a strainer or slotted spoon to pick up the okra, letting excess oil drip into the pot, then transfer the okra to the plate lined with paper towels. Repeat with remaining okra. When finished, turn the heat off and let the oil cool completely. You can save the oil to use again.

■ Preheat a wok over medium-high heat until wisps of smoke rise from the surface. Add 1 teaspoon vegetable oil and let heat for a few seconds until the surface of the oil starts to shimmer. Add the green onions, ginger, garlic, dried chilies, and goji and quickly stir. The goal is to release the fragrance of the aromatics but not burn them. Do this for a few seconds. Add the okra and stir-fry for 10 to 20 seconds to combine the aromatics. Drizzle on the soy sauce and stir-fry again for about 30 seconds, or until the okra are well coated with the sauce. Sprinkle on the sugar and stir again. Turn off the heat. Add the sesame oil, give it one last toss, then transfer to a serving dish. If you're not serving this as a side dish, serve with rice.

> MOM SAYS: It might seem like frozen okra could work, but it's not a good idea to throw a bunch of frozen okra coins into a pot of hot oil. And when defrosted, the okra pieces still contain moisture that doesn't play nicely with oil. Stick with fresh okra.

幸
福
饗
宴

乾煸四季豆

DRY-FRIED GREEN BEANS

VEGAN

EFFORT ●●○

MAKES 4 SERVINGS, FAMILY STYLE

12 ounces French-style green beans or regular green beans

Vegetable oil, for frying

1 green onion, finely chopped

1 teaspoon finely minced or grated fresh ginger

1 large clove garlic, crushed or finely minced

1½ tablespoons soy sauce

1 teaspoon sugar

½ teaspoon sesame oil

This is the most-requested dish at dinner parties. It's savory and slightly caramelized. It's the only way to make green beans as far as we're concerned. While this version is meatless and mild, you can add a bit of ground pork or beef and hot sauce, if you'd like. Some versions include dried shrimp. We keep it straightforward because it's so good as is.

■ Trim the stems off the green beans and cut the beans in half. Line a dinner plate or a large bowl with two layers of paper towels. Set aside.

■ In a 4-quart Dutch oven or similar, add vegetable oil to a depth of 1 inch. Heat on medium to 350 degrees F. In batches, add the green beans and fry for 1 to 2 minutes, or until the skins on the beans wrinkle. Use a strainer or slotted spoon to pick up the beans, letting excess oil drip into the pot, then transfer the beans to the plate lined with paper towels. Repeat with the remaining beans. When finished, turn the heat off and let the oil cool completely. You can save the oil to use again.

■ Preheat a wok over medium-high heat until wisps of smoke rise from the surface. Add 1 teaspoon vegetable oil and let heat for a few seconds until the surface of the oil starts to shimmer. Add the green onions, ginger, and garlic, and quickly stir. The goal is to release the fragrance of the aromatics but not burn them. Do this for a few seconds. Add the beans and stir-fry for 10 to 20 seconds to combine the aromatics. Drizzle on the soy sauce and stir-fry again for about 30 seconds, or until the beans are well coated with the sauce. Sprinkle on the sugar and stir again. Turn off the heat. Add the sesame oil, give it one last toss, then transfer to a serving dish. If you're not serving this as a side dish, serve with rice.

MOM SAYS: If you have my cookbook *Vegetarian Chinese Soul Food*, look up the Dry-Fried Brussels Sprouts recipe. It helped change the minds of at least a couple brussels sprouts haters. That recipe includes diced shiitake mushrooms for extra umami goodness.

假
日
節
慶
小
碟

When you buy Chinese chives, you get a generous bunch. And because Chinese chives are so long, it takes a while to get through them. This recipe was the serendipitous result of needing to use up chives and a bounty of mushrooms.

韭菜炒蘑菇
CHINESE CHIVES
with Mushrooms

VEGAN
EFFORT ●○○
MAKES 4 SERVINGS, FAMILY STYLE

- If you have mushrooms such as beech or enoki, you will need to segment them by trimming off the roots and then gently prying the stems apart. If you have mushrooms such as shiitake or oyster, you will need to slice them into bite-size pieces. Set aside.

- Preheat a wok over high heat until wisps of smoke rise from the surface. Add the vegetable oil and heat for a few seconds until the surface starts to shimmer. Add the chives and stir-fry for about 30 seconds to release the aromas. Add the mushrooms and stir-fry for 1 to 2 minutes to combine with the chives and cook down. Add the soy sauce and stir-fry for 1 more minute. Add the sesame oil and white pepper. Toss one last time, then transfer to a serving dish. If you're not serving this as a side dish, serve with rice.

3 cups assorted mushrooms, such as brown beech, enoki, shiitake, oyster, or your favorite varieties

2 teaspoons vegetable oil

1 cup roughly chopped (2-inch segments) Chinese chives

1 tablespoon soy sauce

½ teaspoon sesame oil

¼ teaspoon white pepper powder (optional)

MOM SAYS: To store Chinese chives, trim off the root end, then cut the leaves into two or three big segments—in order to fit them into a 1-gallon ziplock bag. This helps to keep the pungent aroma from taking over your refrigerator and also makes the chives more manageable.

假日節慶小碟

乾燒抱子甘藍

WOK-CHARRED BRUSSELS SPROUTS
with Smoked Soy Sauce

If you've never had smoked soy sauce, it's worth trying. It adds great dimension to the brussels sprouts. While brussels sprouts are available year-round, the fall is when you can find them in abundance, sometimes even on the branches. That's fresh!

■ To trim the brussels sprouts, cut off the stem end and peel away any rough outer leaves. Set a sprout on the flat stem end. Slice each sprout into ¼-inch-thick pieces. Set aside. Combine the garlic and soy sauce in a small dish. Set aside.

■ Preheat a wok over high heat until wisps of smoke rise from the surface. Add the vegetable oil and let heat for a few seconds until the surface starts to shimmer. Add the brussels sprouts and, using a wok spatula, spread them into a single layer. Let sear for 20 to 30 seconds, or until some of the edges start to char. Stir-fry for a few seconds and let sear for another 10 to 15 seconds. Add the garlic and soy sauce mix. Stir-fry for about 1 minute, or until the sprouts are evenly coated with sauce. Transfer to a serving dish. If you're not serving this as a side dish, serve with rice.

VEGAN

EFFORT ●○○

MAKES 4 SERVINGS, FAMILY STYLE

1 pound brussels sprouts

2 cloves garlic, finely minced or crushed

1½ tablespoons smoked soy sauce

2 tablespoons vegetable oil

MOM SAYS: It's okay if you can't easily find smoked soy sauce. It can be expensive too. This will work with regular soy sauce, of course.

幸
福
饗
宴

蒜香茄子
GARLIC EGGPLANT

VEGAN

EFFORT ●○○

MAKES 4 SERVINGS, FAMILY STYLE

12 ounces Chinese eggplant

1 tablespoon soy sauce

1 tablespoon water

1 tablespoon balsamic vinegar

1 teaspoon grated or finely minced ginger

1 teaspoon crushed garlic

1 green onion, finely chopped

1 teaspoon vegetable oil

½ teaspoon sesame oil

Eggplant can take on so many flavors, you'll never get bored. This is a basic recipe for garlic eggplant that you can push in different directions depending on what it's accompanying. If you need to kick up the spice, add chili sauce or a chili crisp. Not enough garlic? Add as much as you wish. You can top with chopped cilantro for some freshness.

■ Trim the stem end off the eggplants. To cut into batons, first cut the eggplant crosswise into two or three sections. Then cut each section in half lengthwise and each half into 1-inch-wide batons. The length of the batons might vary according to how long the eggplant is, but 3 to 4 inches is about right. Set aside.

■ In a small bowl, combine the soy sauce, water, vinegar, ginger, garlic, and green onion. Set aside.

■ Preheat a wok over high heat until wisps of smoke rise from the surface. Swirl in the vegetable oil and let heat for a few seconds. Add the eggplant to the wok and spread into a single layer. Let char for about 1 minute. Stir-fry for about 15 seconds and then spread into a single layer again. Let char for another minute. Stir-fry for a few seconds, then add the sauce mixture. Stir-fry to coat the eggplant with the sauce, 1 to 2 minutes, or until the eggplant has softened. Drizzle with the sesame oil. Transfer to a serving dish. If you're not serving this as a side dish, serve with rice.

> **MOM SAYS:** If you can't find Chinese eggplants, you can use regular globe eggplants. They're bigger, so you may need only one eggplant. But you can cut them similarly into batons. Also, the skin can be thicker and tougher, so consider shaving it off with a sharp knife before cutting the flesh into batons.

假
日
節
慶
小
碟

This is a dish you can't mess up. Let the cabbage cook down in broth until it's creamy. Hit it with salt or soy sauce and it's done. You can layer in other flavors, sure, but then it would mask the natural sweetness of the cabbage. If you can get to a well-stocked Asian market, try this with baby Chinese cabbage. Cut the baby cabbage heads in half, cut out the core, and then braise the leaves whole. It's comforting.

清炒大白菜
BRAISED CHINESE CABBAGE

EFFORT ●○○

MAKES 4 SERVINGS, FAMILY STYLE

5 cups roughly chopped (2- to 3-inch pieces) Chinese cabbage

4 cups Chinese-Style Chicken Broth (page 226) or water

1 teaspoon soy sauce

1 teaspoon kosher salt, plus more as needed

■ In a medium pot over high heat, combine the cabbage with the broth. Bring to a boil, then reduce the heat to medium-low and simmer for about 15 minutes, stirring occasionally. Add the soy sauce and salt. Stir. Let cook for another 15 minutes, stirring occasionally. If needed, reduce the heat to low. You want a gentle simmer. Taste the liquid for seasoning and add additional salt to taste. Once the cabbage is soft and almost creamy, the dish is done. Transfer to a shallow bowl. If you're not serving this as a side dish, serve with rice.

> **MOM SAYS:** This dish seems bland, but it's not. It's delicate. American palates expect loud, intense flavors. There are many Chinese dishes that are delicate and subtle, so you have to quiet your senses and appreciate a different volume of flavor.

幸
福
饗
宴

燒蘿蔔
BRAISED DAIKON

VEGAN

EFFORT ●○○

MAKES 4 SERVINGS, FAMILY STYLE

1 pound daikon, peeled and cut into 2-inch chunks

4 cups water

2 tablespoons soy sauce

¼ cup fried shallots

Kosher salt

It's true that daikon announce their presence in your kitchen when you cook them. But they are so delicious, and this recipe, while elemental, showcases the natural flavors of daikon. It's a set-it-and-forget-it dish, which we love. Especially if you're making a big feast, you want dishes that aren't demanding to balance out the ones that are. You also can use Korean radish, which is wider and squatter than daikon.

■ In a medium pot over high heat, combine the daikon, water, and soy sauce. Bring to a boil, then reduce the heat to low. Let the daikon simmer for 30 minutes, stirring occasionally. Add the fried shallots and let simmer for 10 to 15 minutes more, or until the daikon is tender and has some translucence. Taste the broth. If needed, add salt to taste. Transfer to a serving bowl. If you're not serving this as a side dish, serve with rice.

MOM SAYS: You can enrich the broth by adding a few Chinese dried red dates, which bring in a touch of sweetness and TCM (traditional Chinese medicine) qualities. Dried red dates, or jujubes, help balance your body's qi, or life force. Also, if you're an omnivore, you can use Chinese-Style Chicken Broth (page 226) instead of water to enrich the flavor.

Escarole shows up more in Italian cooking and isn't a part of the Chinese produce spectrum, but it certainly holds its own in stir-fries. The leaves have a hint of bitterness, which breaks up the umami richness of the mushrooms and soy sauce.

清炒冬菇生菜
STIR-FRIED ESCAROLE
with Shiitake

VEGAN
EFFORT ●○○
MAKES 4 SERVINGS, FAMILY STYLE

1 pound escarole

1 tablespoon soy sauce

3 cloves garlic, finely minced or crushed

1 teaspoon Chinese black vinegar or balsamic vinegar

1 tablespoon vegetable oil

4 medium dried shiitake mushrooms, soaked in warm water for 2 to 3 hours, sliced ¼ inch thick (about ½ cup sliced)

½ teaspoon sesame oil

⅛ teaspoon white pepper powder (optional)

- Cut the escarole into quarters lengthwise through the core. Cut out the core. Slice the quarters crosswise into pieces that are about 1½ inches wide. This doesn't have to be exact. What's important is that the pieces are relatively the same size. You should have about 4 packed cups. Set aside.

- In a small bowl, combine the soy sauce, garlic, and vinegar.

- Preheat a wok over high heat until wisps of smoke rise from the surface. Add the vegetable oil and let heat for a few seconds until the surface starts to shimmer. Add the shiitake and let sear for about 30 seconds. Add the escarole and stir-fry for about 2 minutes, or until the leafy parts start to wilt and no longer look raw. Swirl in the sauce mixture and stir-fry for 1 minute. Add the sesame oil and white pepper. Give it one last stir to combine. Turn off the heat and transfer to a serving dish. If you're not serving this as a side dish, serve with rice.

MOM SAYS: Trying to remember that you have to rehydrate dried ingredients like shiitake mushrooms is sometimes hard. You can use fresh shiitake, if that's easier. But I prefer the more intense flavor of the dried mushroom.

幸
福
饗
宴

清炒枸杞羽衣甘藍
STIR-FRIED KALE
with Dried Cranberries

VEGAN

EFFORT ● ○ ○

MAKES 4 SERVINGS, FAMILY STYLE

1 bunch Tuscan kale (about 8 ounces)

¼ teaspoon kosher salt

1 teaspoon vegetable oil

½ cup dried sweetened cranberries

1 tablespoon water

1 teaspoon soy sauce

½ teaspoon grated fresh ginger

2 tablespoons fried shallots

Kale is so popular, we wanted to include it in a recipe. Around Thanksgiving, people start thinking about different ways to use cranberries. Both come together for this stir-fry, which is savory and sweet and looks festive. We prefer Tuscan kale, which is also known as dinosaur kale.

■ Remove the stems from the kale. There are two ways you can do so: The first is to take one stem of kale, fold the leaves together to expose the stem, and lay the kale on the cutting board, with the stem side facing your knife. Carefully glide the tip of your knife along the edge of the stem, separating it from the leaf. Repeat with the other stems. Discard or compost the stems; do not put them in the garbage disposal. The second option is to hold the stem with the leaf tip facing down. With your thumb and fingers of the opposite hand, grip the stem above where the leaf starts. Glide your fingers down the stem with a little force to tear the leaf away from the rib. Repeat with the remaining leaves.

■ Gather the leaves. They will be unruly, but gather a few leaves together and cut them into 2-inch sections. Place in a bowl and repeat with the remaining kale leaves. Sprinkle the salt on the cut leaves and work in the salt while bruising the leaves. Do this for about 1 minute. Set aside.

■ Preheat a wok over high heat until wisps of smoke rise from the surface. Add the vegetable oil and let heat for a few seconds until the surface starts to shimmer. Add the kale leaves and stir-fry for about 30 seconds. Add the cranberries, water, soy sauce, and ginger. Stir-fry for about 1 minute, or until the kale leaves have wilted slightly. Transfer to a serving dish. Sprinkle on the fried shallots. If you're not serving this as a side dish, serve with rice.

MOM SAYS: My mother, Meilee's lau lau, likes this dish. She enjoys the hit of tart sweetness that cranberries add to balance the hearty flavor of kale. Approval from Grandma is a good thing.

幸
福
饗
宴

酸辣台灣高麗菜
HOT-AND-SOUR TAIWANESE CABBAGE

VEGAN

EFFORT ●○○

MAKES 4 SERVINGS, FAMILY STYLE

About 1 pound wedge Taiwanese cabbage (usually about a quarter of a large head, or roughly 6 cups cut or torn)

2 cloves garlic, crushed

1 tablespoon soy sauce

1 tablespoon water

1 teaspoon chili crisp

1 teaspoon Chinese black vinegar or balsamic vinegar

½ teaspoon grated fresh ginger

1 tablespoon vegetable oil

Taiwanese cabbage looks like a larger, flattened version of a regular green cabbage. There's always a head of Taiwanese cabbage in the refrigerator that we can stir-fry quickly as a side dish. We love it! You do have to go to an Asian market to find Taiwanese cabbage, however. The cabbage can be quite large and some stores sell them in halves. Sometimes there are smaller heads. Either way, you won't use a whole cabbage all at once. It usually takes us a few meals to get through one cabbage. It's okay because they hold well in the fridge. If you can't get to an Asian market, you can try this recipe with green cabbage.

■ If you have a wedge of cabbage that contains the core, cut it out. Cut the cabbage into roughly 1-inch squares. Or, if you want a less uniform look, you can tear the leaves into relatively bite-size pieces. Either way works. Set aside.

■ In a small bowl, combine the garlic, soy sauce, water, chili crisp, vinegar, and ginger. Set aside.

■ Preheat a wok over high heat until wisps of smoke rise from the surface. Swirl in the oil and let heat for a few seconds until the surface starts to shimmer. Add the cabbage leaves and spread into a single layer. Let sear until you get a bit of char, about 30 seconds. Stir-fry for a few seconds to shift the cabbage, and then let the leaves sear for 15 seconds. Stir-fry for a few more seconds, then add the sauce mixture. Stir-fry to coat the leaves with the sauce and cook through, 1 to 2 minutes. Transfer to a serving dish. If you're not serving this as a side dish, serve with rice.

MOM SAYS: You can adjust the level of pungency by adding more or less chili crisp, garlic, and ginger. You also can add fresh chili peppers or dried red chilies. It's flexible and is a great canvas for different combinations of spices. Of course, you can always skip the spice if you want it mild.

清炒土豆絲
STIR-FRIED SHOESTRING POTATOES

VEGAN

EFFORT ●○○

MAKES 4 SERVINGS, FAMILY STYLE

12 ounces waxy potatoes, such as red potatoes, peeled

2 cloves garlic, crushed

2 tablespoons water

1 teaspoon unseasoned rice vinegar

½ teaspoon soy sauce

½ teaspoon kosher salt

1 tablespoon vegetable oil

2 dried red chilies, cut with scissors into ½-inch segments

½ teaspoon sesame oil

¼ teaspoon white pepper powder

Back in the 1990s, this stir-fried potato dish was on the menu at our family's Chinese restaurant. Customers were surprised that potatoes could be stir-fried and that they would taste so delicious. In more recent years, this dish has become common on many Chinese restaurant menus, though we're not sure if folks know there's a simple treasure hiding in plain sight. It's essential that you cut the potatoes into fine threads. Too chunky and the dish loses some of its magic.

■ If you have a mandoline, you can use it to cut the potatoes into fine julienne, about ⅛ inch thick. If you don't have a mandoline, use a sharp knife to cut ⅛-inch-thick slices of potato, lengthwise. Then shingle the slices (or make a small stack of two or three slices) and cut into fine ⅛-inch strips. Place in a bowl with enough cold water to cover. Repeat with the rest of the potatoes. Let soak in the water for about 10 minutes. Then strain the potatoes in a colander, shaking off any excess water. Set aside.

■ In a small bowl, stir together the garlic, water, rice vinegar, soy sauce, and salt. Set aside.

■ Preheat a wok over high heat until wisps of smoke rise from the surface. Swirl in the vegetable oil. Add the red chilies and stir for a few seconds, but not too long, because you don't want to burn them. Add the potatoes and immediately start stir-frying to mix with the chilies, about 1 minute. Add the sauce mixture and stir-fry for about 3 minutes, or until the potatoes are cooked but still slightly firm. Drizzle on the sesame oil and sprinkle on the white pepper. Give it one last stir and transfer to a serving dish. If you're not serving this as a side dish, serve with rice.

MOM SAYS: For color, you can mix in some fine strips of carrots. Some versions include bell peppers, but I prefer it with just potatoes.

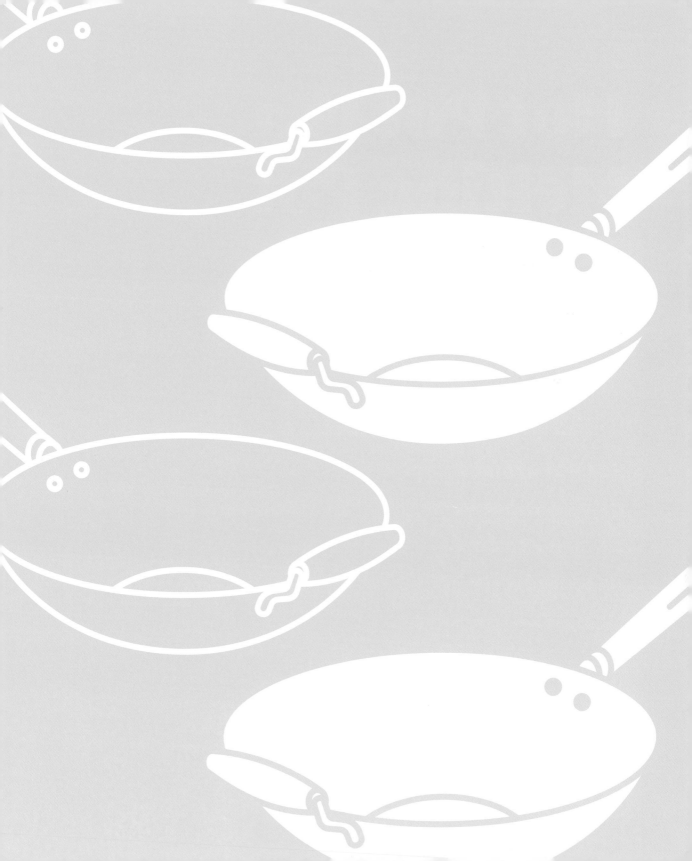

Hot Pot Is a Melting Pot

SIMMERING GOODNESS

We have more memories around hot pots than we can recount. But there are moments through the years that pop into our respective minds. For Hsiao-Ching, it's late-night hot pot dinners sitting around the coffee table at the Wilson Avenue house in Columbia, Missouri. The hot pot was a red electric wok—which never was used as a wok—and the Chinese cabbage, frozen tofu, bean thread, and fish balls were abundant. For Meilee, it's getting together with cousins for a birthday, or just because, at different hot pot restaurants around Seattle. Some casual, some high-end, always with generous amounts of ingredients and copious laughter.

We wanted to bring that spirit into this chapter. It can be expensive to go out to a hot pot restaurant, especially these days. Whether hot pot night is its own occasion or the backdrop for a celebration, you can host it with some light assembling of components. Or make it potluck-style and have everyone contribute an ingredient or two. Having a hot pot party is the best of all worlds. You get to be independent and choose your ingredients to then dip into a communal cauldron of broth. A hot pot, thus, is a melting pot in more ways than one.

EQUIPMENT

Hot Pot

The two main styles are electric and butane. Both are widely available at Asian markets or online. The benefit to electric hot pots is that they're electric, but they can be expensive at $70 to $100 or more. Butane stoves are common in restaurants. The burners and fuel canisters are inexpensive—about $20 for a burner—and plentiful at Asian markets. But the drawback is that they use butane and the stove creates an open fire. That may not be ideal in some situations. Which should you get? We have both kinds. The electric pot is a good bet because it doesn't require buying cans of butane fuel.

Tools

Bowls, plates, chopsticks, soup spoons, wire ladles or tongs, and dipping bowls.

INGREDIENTS

Assorted Vegetables

It's your choice what vegetables to include. These are some common vegetables ideal for hot pot:

- Chinese cabbage
- Baby bok choy
- Spinach
- Tung ho (chrysanthemum leaves)
- Mushrooms (shiitake, enoki, etc.)
- Daikon
- Bean sprouts
- Corn
- Snow peas
- Tofu
- Tomatoes
- Assorted meats and seafood

Asian markets sell thinly sliced meats of all grades and cuts for hot pot (also called shabu-shabu in Japanese). Choose an assortment of what you like.

- Pork (shoulder)
- Beef (short rib, rib eye, brisket, eye of round)
- Chicken (breast)
- Lamb (shoulder)
- Shrimp (in the shell and, ideally, with the head on)
- Fish (tilapia is common, but we prefer branzino or halibut)
- Fish balls and/or fish cake
- Beef meatballs
- Accompaniments

You definitely want rice or noodles. As with meats and vegetables, choose what you like in your soup.

- Rice
- Instant noodles
- Bean thread
- Frozen dumplings
- Kimchi
- Preserved Chinese mustard greens
- Sichuan pickled vegetables

Broth

You can make your own broth, and we've got some recipes in this chapter. You can also choose one of the soup base packets from any number of makers, including from chain hot pot restaurants such as Happy Lamb, Haidilao, and Boiling Point. If you're a fan of any of these and other chains, you can mimic the flavors with their packaged soup bases. The caveat is that these packets also contain a lot of preservatives. But they are convenient!

Sauce Bar

Create a small condiment bar so your guests can mix their own dipping sauces. Here are some suggestions for sauces you can buy and then mix and match. You probably already have soy sauce, hoisin sauce, and a chili crisp or other hot sauce. It really doesn't have to be more complicated than that. For the adventurous, try XO sauce or fermented tofu (which comes in jars in the condiment aisle).

Hot	Sour	Salty	Sweet	Funky	Nutty	Aromatic
• Chili Crisp	• Black Vinegar	• Soy Sauce	• Hoisin Sauce	• Fermented Tofu	• Sesame Paste	• Scallion Oil
• Chili Sauce	• Rice Vinegar	• Oyster Sauce	• Dumpling Sauce	• Sacha Sauce	• Sesame Oil	• Garlic Oil
• Chili Oil	• Katsu Sauce	• Bean Sauce	• Sweet Chili Sauce	• XO Sauce		
		• Black Bean Garlic Sauce	• Japanese Barbecue Sauce			

BACHAN'S ORIGINAL JAPANESE
BARBECUE SAUCE

XO SAUCE

THAI SWEET
CHILI SAUCE

LEE KUM KEE
HOISIN SAUCE

LEE KUM KEE BLACK
PEPPER SAUCE

FLY BY JING
ZHONG SAUCE

LEE KUM KEE BLACK
BEAN GARLIC SAUCE

BULL-DOG
TONKATSU SAUCE

CHILI CRISP

JUAN CHENG
PIXIAN CHILI
BEAN PASTE

FERMENTED
TOFU

BULLHEAD SACHA SAUCE

幸
福
饗
宴

MEILEE'S PERSPECTIVE: SCENES FROM HOT POT

We've had a lot of hot pot through the years! No matter the celebration, hot pot is one of my family's go-to meals. (The other is going out for soup dumplings.) The grown-ups go for the more sophisticated ingredients like squid and shrimp with the head on or the super-spicy broth. My cousins and I tend to go for milder foods. Sometimes, what we like best isn't even for dipping in broth, like the deep-fried steamed buns at Haidilao. We can eat a lot of those! Whether it's at home, in the fanciest shop in town, or at a mom-and-pop, a night of hot pot with our family is always full of love.

This is a mild broth that pairs well with vegetables. If you prefer more kick, you can either add spice to this recipe or use the Mushroom-Tomato Broth (page 230). There are many more vegetable options than listed here, so explore the produce aisle for other greens you might like to try in a hot pot.

■ To make the broth, in a large soup pot, combine the water, kelp, bean sprouts, shiitake mushrooms, celery, ginger, green onions, and dates. Bring to a boil, reduce the heat to low, and let simmer for about 20 minutes. Strain the broth and season to taste with kosher salt.

■ Transfer broth to the hot pot and bring to a simmer. Start dipping your ingredients when the broth is ready.

> MOM SAYS: We're all so used to seeing the spiciest hot pots represented in food media that a mild version seems unexciting. Sometimes, it's the simplest dishes that celebrate the natural flavors of ingredients.

素菜鍋
VEGETARIAN HOT POT

火鍋～～多元總會

VEGAN

EFFORT ●○○

MAKES 4 TO 6 SERVINGS, FAMILY STYLE

FOR THE BROTH:

10 cups water

2 squares dried kelp or kombu (about 1 gram)

½ cup bean sprouts

4 medium dried shiitake mushrooms

1 rib celery heart (light-green inner stalk), halved

2 slices fresh ginger, about ¼ inch thick and 3 inches long

2 green onions, cut into 3-inch segments

4 Chinese dried red dates

Kosher salt

FOR THE VEGETABLES:

2 cups sliced Chinese cabbage

2 cups sliced baby bok choy

2 cups baby spinach leaves

2 cups sliced daikon

2 cups assorted mushrooms

2 bundles bean thread, soaked in warm water to soften

FOR SERVING:

Dipping sauces (see Sauce Bar page 222)

Rice

幸
福
饗
宴

高湯
CHINESE-STYLE CHICKEN BROTH

EFFORT ●○○

MAKES ABOUT 8 CUPS

2 to 3 pounds chicken bones and drumsticks or whatever cuts you prefer (use a mix of bones and a bit of meat for flavor)

12 cups water, plus more as needed

2 green onions, halved

3 big slices fresh ginger, about ¼ inch thick and 3 inches long

3 tablespoons soy sauce

¼ cup Shaoxing rice wine or an everyday white wine, such as pinot grigio or sauvignon blanc

6 medium dried shiitake mushrooms

3 large Chinese dried red dates (optional)

1 teaspoon kosher salt, plus more as needed

Whenever we need chicken for a stir-fry, katsu, or curry, we start with a whole chicken and break it down. That means there will be a carcass, wings, thigh bones, and drumsticks that will go in a pot with water and aromatics to simmer for hours. You don't have to do it this way, of course. You can buy chicken parts or, if you can get to an Asian market, the butcher counter usually sells packs of chicken carcasses for broth. Unlike Western-style chicken broths, which use onions, celery, carrots, thyme, bay leaves, parsley, and such, Chinese broth uses green onions, ginger, rice wine, and shiitake to build flavor.

■ Place the chicken bones and parts in a large stockpot with the water. If needed, add more water to make sure the bones are covered by 1 inch of water. Bring to a boil over high heat. Reduce heat to low. Using a fine-mesh strainer or skimmer, skim off the scum that floats on the surface. Let simmer for about 15 minutes and skim again. Repeat this process several times in the first hour. Once you've cleared the foamy bits, you'll start to see rendered chicken fat on the surface. Some folks like to keep the fat. We skim off the large pools of fat so there isn't a grease slick when we taste the broth.

■ At the 1-hour mark, add the green onions, ginger, soy sauce, rice wine, shiitake mushrooms, and red dates. Gently stir to make sure the aromatics are distributed in the broth. Continue to simmer for an hour. Taste the broth, then add the salt, stir, and taste again. Repeat this until the broth tastes balanced. Before using the broth, carefully pour it through a fine-mesh strainer to catch any remaining scum or bits. If saving for later, refrigerate for up to 3 days, or divide into freezer containers and freeze.

> MOM SAYS: This broth is versatile. It's so soothing on its own with some rice. It also is the base of my wonton soup and various braises.

火
鍋
～
～
多
元
總
會

This is adaptable to your personal taste and spice tolerance. If you want it incendiary, then add as much spice as you want. This recipe is a starting point. The optional preserved mustard greens is a pickle and adds a hit of acidity. If you do add the pickle, note that you may not need to add extra salt.

■ Add the broth to the hot pot. Stir in the chili crisp, soy sauce, star anise, red chilies, Sichuan peppercorns, and mustard greens. Bring to a low boil, reduce heat, and start dipping your ingredients. If needed, you can add salt to taste.

> **MOM SAYS:** Use a chili crisp that has plenty of oil. Adding the oil to the broth will bathe your ingredients in flavor.

辣味鍋
SPICY BROTH

EFFORT ●○○
MAKES ABOUT 8 CUPS

8 cups Chinese-Style Chicken Broth (page 226) or homemade or store-bought vegetable broth

4 tablespoons chili crisp with oil

2 tablespoons soy sauce

1 star anise

6 dried red chili peppers

1 teaspoon Sichuan peppercorns

1 cup sliced preserved Chinese mustard greens (optional)

Kosher salt

幸
福
饗
宴

蕃茄蘑菇鍋
MUSHROOM-TOMATO BROTH

VEGAN

EFFORT ●○○

MAKES ABOUT 8 CUPS

2 teaspoons vegetable oil

1 cup diced fresh tomatoes

2 tablespoons soy sauce

8 cups water

2 green onions, cut into 3-inch segments

2 slices fresh ginger, about ¼ inch thick and 3 inches long

6 medium dried shiitake mushrooms

Kosher salt

This base is how we start tomato egg drop soup. The combination of soy sauce and tomatoes creates a magical flavor. You can use any type of tomato, but if heirloom tomatoes are in season, use those. Otherwise, Roma or Campari tomatoes work fine. In a pinch, you could use canned diced tomatoes.

■ In a large soup pot, heat the vegetable oil over medium heat. Add the tomatoes and cook, stirring, for about 1 minute. Add the soy sauce and stir. Let cook for about 30 seconds, stirring to keep the tomatoes from sticking too much. Add the water, green onions, ginger, and dried mushrooms, and stir. Let simmer over low heat for about 30 minutes, or until the mushrooms are rehydrated and cooked through.

■ Transfer the broth to the hot pot, bring to a simmer, and start dipping your ingredients.

MOM SAYS: If you don't mind chicken broth, you can start with that instead of water.

火
鍋
～

～
多
元
總
會

While this recipe includes meat, you can make a yin-yang hot pot vegetarian by using the Mushroom-Tomato Broth (page 230) or the Spicy Broth (page 227) made with vegetable broth instead of chicken. And add more vegetables and vegetarian proteins instead of meat. Of course, feel free to substitute or add your favorite ingredients.

■ Place the broths in a hot pot that has a divider. Bring to a simmer. Meanwhile, set the other ingredients around the hot pot and start dipping when the broth comes to temperature.

> MOM SAYS: I love having two broth options because, in our family, we each have a different level of spice tolerance.

陰陽鍋
YIN-YANG HOT POT

EFFORT ●○○

MAKES 4 TO 6 SERVINGS, FAMILY STYLE

8 cups Chinese-Style Chicken Broth (page 226) or store-bought, plus more broth or hot water as needed

8 cups Spicy Broth (page 227), plus more broth or hot water as needed

4 to 6 cups sliced Chinese cabbage or a mix of Asian leafy greens, such as bok choy, ong choy, or spinach

1 package (about 8 ounces) fish balls or fish cake

2 cups mushrooms, such as shiitake, enoki, beech, or your choice

1 package (about 16 ounces) soft or medium-firm tofu, cut into 1-inch pieces

1 to 2 bundles bean thread, soaked in warm water to soften

12 to 16 ounces assorted meats, sliced for hot pot

FOR SERVING:

Dipping sauces (see Sauce Bar page 222)

Rice

幸
福
饗
宴

肉湯鍋
MEAT LOVER'S HOT POT

EFFORT ●○○

MAKES 4 TO 6 SERVINGS, FAMILY STYLE

8 cups Chinese-Style Chicken Broth (page 226) or Spicy Broth (page 227), plus more broth or hot water as needed

6 to 8 ounces beef rib eye, sliced for hot pot

4 ounces Wagyu eye of round, sliced for hot pot

6 to 8 ounces Kurobuta pork butt, sliced for hot pot

4 ounces pork belly, sliced for hot pot

4 ounces chicken breast, sliced for hot pot

2 cups sliced Chinese cabbage or baby bok choy leaves

FOR SERVING:

Dipping sauces (see Sauce Bar page 222)

Rice

There used to be a contemporary Korean barbecue restaurant in Seattle that offered a "baller" tower of meats for the grill. We could have borrowed that term for this recipe, but who knows what slang word will be trendy when you read this. The point is that you can assemble a carnivorous feast limited only by your budget. The particular cuts and quantities are up to you, but we get you started here. You can use one broth or two for a yin-yang hot pot, or substitute store-bought if you wish.

■ Place broth in the hot pot and bring to a simmer. Meanwhile, set the other ingredients around the hot pot and start dipping when the broth comes to temperature.

MOM SAYS: I know this is for meat lovers and we did add cabbage, but you should consider adding some other vegetable as well.

When a broth is loaded with seafood goodness, we describe the flavor in Mandarin as xiān (鲜), which is that umami richness. It's important that the seafood you buy is super, super fresh. If the seafood is off even the slightest, it will affect the experience of this hot pot. Remember not to overcook any of the seafood; you want the texture to remain delicate and succulent.

■ To devein the shrimp: Starting on the end opposite the tail, use scissors to cut into the back of the shrimp about ⅛ inch deep. Cut only to the where the body starts to taper to the tail. Once you have created this slit, you should be able to see the black vein. Rinse under cold water as you remove the vein. Place the shrimp in a bowl. Repeat with the remaining shrimp. Set aside.

■ Place the broth in a hot pot and bring to a simmer. Add the clams and the fish balls. The clams are ready to eat when they open. The fish balls will puff up when they're heated through and ready to eat. Dip the shrimp, fish, and other ingredients as desired.

> **MOM SAYS:** You could also include crab in the shell. Some hot pot restaurants include surimi ("krab" meat, a.k.a. white fish made to look like crab). You can too, if you like surimi. It's not my taste, however.

海鮮鍋
SEAFOOD HOT POT

火鍋 ～ ～ 多元總會

EFFORT ●○○

MAKES 4 TO 6 SERVINGS, FAMILY STYLE

8 ounces headless shrimp in the shell (31/35 size)

8 cups Chinese-Style Chicken Broth (page 226) or Spicy Broth (page 227), plus more broth or hot water as needed

1 pound clams, scrubbed

8 ounces fish balls with roe

½ to 1 pound fish fillet, such as halibut, snapper, branzino, or your choice

2 cups sliced Chinese cabbage

1 small pack beech mushrooms (about 3 ounces)

2 bundles bean thread, soaked in warm water to soften

FOR SERVING:

Dipping sauces (see Sauce Bar page 222)

Rice

Resources

Huang, Shu-Chun. "Intentions for the Recreational Use of Public Landscaped Cemeteries in Taiwan." *Landscape Research* 32, no. 2 (2007): 207–223.

Huang, Su Huei. *Chinese Snacks: Wei-Chuan Cooking Book.* Taipei: Wei-Chuan Publishing Co., 1974.

Lau, Theodora. *The Handbook of Chinese Horoscopes*. 4th ed. New York: Harper Perennial, 2000.

Moey, S. C. *Chinese Feasts & Festivals: A Cookbook.* Singapore: Periplus, 2006.

"The Crowded Cemeteries of Hong Kong—in Pictures." TheGuardian.com, January 21, 2015.

Wei, Liming. *Chinese Festivals*. 3rd ed. Cambridge: Cambridge University Press, 2011.

Acknowledgments

MOM SAYS: Thank you, Meilee, for collaborating with me on this book and for baring your insights and personal truths. I cherish the micro-moments we've shared during this experience. Eating delivery dim sum in a New York hotel room on a bunk bed after a weeklong photo shoot comes to mind. I can hear in my mind the pride and, perhaps, triumph that filled your voice when you read out loud to me your essay on your name. May this book and the effort it culminates serve you well in your endeavors to come.

Thank you to Eric, Shen, and my mother, Ellen, for being patient with me as I focused on Meilee and juggled meeting the deadline for the manuscript with working my day job. I was not always present in a given moment and I definitely wasn't patient in return. You each played your parts in making this book a reality. While writing is a solitary act, making a book is not. PS: Eric, thank you for a comedy-filled September. "Let's watch a show."

Thank you to the extended Chou family that includes my brothers, sister-in-law, nieces, and nephews: Sam, David, Alisha, Jackson, Lucie, Sadie, Duncan, and Fletcher. It's such a privilege to be able to watch everyone grow. As the kids become more independent, I'm heartened that potstickers, scallion pancakes, pork belly, and so many other flavors always bring us back together.

Thank you, Clare Barboza, for your partnership in creating another beautiful book.

How fun it was to have Joe and Hugo be a part of our New York adventure! Thank you, Joe Barboza, for feeding all of us after our long days in the photo studio and for crossing state lines to get branzino. Ha ha ha!

Thank you to Jill Saginario, our editor at Sasquatch Books, and publisher Jen Worick for coming to that Book Larder event when I interviewed Naomi Duguid and encouraging me to share my idea for book three. You openly welcomed Meilee into the Sasquatch family because you trusted me. That's deeply meaningful and I'm grateful. Of course, the whole Sasquatch team is fantastic: Tony Ong, how great that we've been able to collaborate on designing three books! I appreciate Nikki Sprinkle for marketing my previous books and our new one and making sure these titles stay fresh in people's minds. Managing editor Peggy Gannon has helped keep all of us on track. Erin Cusick's precision as a copyeditor makes me glad she's on our team.

Special thanks to Laura Gatewood and Robert Taylor for contributing to the recipe testing process. Laura, if I could insert the perfect GIPHY here, I would.

MEILEE SAYS: It was a rainy Tuesday night and I had asked my mom to go on a drive with me to Target. Within a few minutes, we had hopped into the car ready for the adventure. I spent the first half of the drive listening to music and

幸
福
饗
宴

looking at the rain dripping down the windows. My mom turned to me at a red light and asked, "Do you want to work on my next book with me?" I sat there, reflecting on the years of watching my mom's creative process for her other books. I thought about her late nights in her office, the meticulous staging of her photos, and the daily kitchen experiments.

At the time, I was a junior in high school, and I wondered whether I was ready for such an endeavor. As I listened to my mom lay out her vision for the book, suggesting what I could contribute and even discussing potential research trips, I found myself in agreement. Throughout the journey of creating this book, I witnessed my mom's incredible ability to whip up feasts in an hour, to write from dusk till dawn, all while juggling a full-time job and

being an unwaveringly supportive parent. She not only motivated me but also introduced me to countless new experiences and invaluable life lessons. She has played a significant role in shaping the person I am today. My deepest gratitude and admiration all go to her. Thank you, Mom.

In addition, I'd like to express my gratitude to our entire family. The moments we've shared have been the inspiration for my writing, and I'm immensely proud to be a part of our family. I'd also like to extend my thanks to our editor, Jill, for helping to guide me through this process and for believing in this book. In sharing a year in my family's life through these essays, recipes, and history, I hope this book serves as a tribute to the moments of love and good food that have brought us together.

Index

Note: Page numbers in *italic* refer to photographs.

About the Authors

HSIAO-CHING CHOU is an award-winning food journalist and author of three cookbooks on Chinese home cooking. Known for her potsticker classes, she has taught hundreds of students over the years. She is the past chair of the James Beard Foundation's Book Awards Committee and serves on the board of directors for the Ballard Food Bank. When she's not wearing her culinary hat, she makes a living as an editorial director in the tech industry. Chou lives with her family in Seattle.

MEILEE CHOU RIDDLE is a student of filmmaking, writing, and music. She comes from a family of storytellers, including her TV producer dad, Eric Riddle; cookbook author mom, Hsiao-Ching Chou; and lifestyle blogger grandma, Ellen Chou. Meilee is always looking for ways to express her creativity. Her award-winning films have been featured in regional and national film festivals. She lives in Seattle with her family.